THE ART OF

OVERWATCH®
VOLUME 2

WILL MURAI

THE ART OF

OVERWATCH®
VOLUME 2

TITAN BOOKS

BLIZZARD
ENTERTAINMENT

CREDITS

Written by
MATT BURNS

Edited by
CHLOE FRABONI and **ALLISON AVALON IRONS**

Designed by
BETSY PETERSCHMIDT

Produced by
BRIANNE MESSINA

Art Consultation by
ARNOLD TSANG and **DION ROGERS**

Lore Consultation by
MADI BUCKINGHAM, SEAN COPELAND, and **JUSTIN PARKER**

Special Thanks
JEFF CHAMBERLAIN, WHITNEY DAY, ADAM GERSHOWITZ, NATALIA GONCHAROVA, and **KIM HORN**

BLIZZARD ENTERTAINMENT

Vice President, Consumer Products
MATTHEW BEECHER

Director, Consumer Products, Publishing
BYRON PARNELL

Associate Publishing Manager
DEREK ROSENBERG

Director, Manufacturing
ANNA WAN

Senior Director, Story and Franchise Development
DAVID SEEHOLZER

Senior Producer
BRIANNE MESSINA

Lead Editor
CHLOE FRABONI

Editor
ALLISON AVALON IRONS

Book Art & Design Manager
BETSY PETERSCHMIDT

Historian Supervisor
SEAN COPELAND

Senior Historian
JUSTIN PARKER

Associate Historian
MADI BUCKINGHAM

Published by Titan Books, London, in 2021.
Published by arrangement with Blizzard Entertainment, Inc., Irvine, California.

TITAN BOOKS
A division of Titan Publishing Group Ltd
144 Southwark Street. London SE1 0UP
www.titanbooks.com
Find us on Facebook: www.facebook.com/titanbooks
Follow us on Twitter: @TitanBooks
A CIP catalogue record for this title is available from the British Library.

Case
ISBN barcode: 978-1-789098-91-4
Manufactured in China

Print run 10 9 8 7 6 5 4 3 2 1

First Edition

CONTENTS

INTRODUCTION

Two important parts of working on *Overwatch* are exploring unique ideas and overcoming the challenges that these ideas inevitably bring (and there are *always* challenges). Case in point: Wrecking Ball, the highly intelligent hamster who pilots an advanced mech. He's one of *Overwatch*'s most unique characters, from both a playstyle and art perspective. When we decided to add him to the game, every member of the team had to figure out how he would fit. Did a whimsical character like that even have a place in *Overwatch*? What should his abilities be? With those little hamster hands controlling the mech, what would he look like in first-person? *How are we going to do it?*

That last question is a pretty familiar one—we face it whenever we design a new hero, environment, or in-game event. In fact, we've been asking ourselves "How are we going to do it?" from the earliest days of the game's development. When *Overwatch* was released on May 24, 2016, it was the first new universe Blizzard Entertainment had created in more than seventeen years. It was also our only first-person shooter, and it featured a bright and colorful art aesthetic different from established titles like *World of Warcraft*, *StarCraft*, and *Diablo*.

NESSKAIN

When we were building the visual direction for *Overwatch* all those years ago, our goal was to go beyond just creating something new; from the beginning, we aimed to create something new *and* familiar. We wanted to imbue *Overwatch* with an aesthetic all its own, but we also wanted to embrace the visual legacy that Blizzard had already established. That way, people who had played our other games would find something familiar— something comforting—in *Overwatch*. When they looked at Reinhardt's big shoulder pads and larger-than-life proportions, they would be reminded of *StarCraft*'s marines or the warriors and paladins from *World of Warcraft*.

We made a point of identifying visual hooks like this— stylistic elements shared between Blizzard's existing games—so we could weave them into the futuristic world of Tracer, Winston, and Reaper. We eventually settled on four guiding art pillars for *Overwatch*. First, creating characters and locations that were diverse, not only in terms of backstory and culture, but in proportions and design language. Second, weaving a vision of the future filled with hope and aspirational themes. Third, making character animations and environments dynamic. And fourth, handcrafting everything from textures to special effects to ensure the world felt made by people rather than simulated by computers.

Figuring out what these pillars were and bringing them to life in *Overwatch* really defined the years leading up to the game's release. But after that big day on May 24, 2016, we faced the challenge of maintaining our collective vision while also pushing our art into exciting new places.

That familiar question was always on our minds: "How are we going to do it?"

It wasn't limited to just art either. After *Overwatch*'s release, we had to figure out where we would take the game next. We knew we wanted to make a sequel—we'd been thinking about it since 2015. Once we had shipped the first game, we had an opportunity to focus on it—but we also wanted to craft live content to support people continuing to play *Overwatch*. An incredible international community had formed around the game—a community that continually inspires us with their creativity and passion—and we were determined to give them the best experience that we could.

So, we found a way to do both. We launched new seasonal events, heroes, environments, sprays, icons, game modes, and more. While we were working on this content, we learned lessons that helped us lay the foundation for *Overwatch 2*.

Many of these lessons related to *Overwatch*'s visual style. In the early days, we were strict about our art style and the way the game was represented. We wanted to imprint upon people that these are our characters and they're from a game called *Overwatch*. For example, whenever we showed Tracer, it had to be a certain way, and she had to point her gun in a certain style. But we always knew if our game was accepted by enough people it would allow us to naturally expand what *Overwatch* art could be. And that was what happened after the game's release. We had this wonderful opportunity to explore new visual possibilities—and we embraced it.

The content in this book, created from mid-2017 onward, chronicles how our approach to art evolved—and how it stayed true to its roots. We were always looking for opportunities to learn and grow, but we made a point of championing the art values and pillars that had helped us bring the game to life.

Because of that shared vision, the art of *Overwatch* all came together.

—THE OVERWATCH TEAM

NESSKAIN

WILL MURAI

HEROES

At its core, *Overwatch* is a story about heroes of all walks of life fighting for our world's future. As these characters express *Overwatch*'s core themes, every hero is designed with meticulous purpose, right down to the way they dress, talk, and move. Their diverse backgrounds give people all over the world something to connect with, while their unique color palettes, animations, and abilities give the heroes an identity all their own.

"Each one feels like a new challenge. They all have slightly different needs, so we're always experimenting, pushing the limits on things, like how abilities feel," said *Overwatch*'s senior art director, Bill Petras. "We wanted to make sure we weren't afraid to take risks."

ABOVE: **NESSKAIN**

By mid-2017, twenty-four heroes were present in the game, and the team planned to add many more in the months and years to come. "You always want to surprise the community by introducing new experiences and characters into the universe," said former concept artist Ben Zhang. "Everyone on the team wanted to experiment with new things. The difficulties and challenges we faced along the way were by-products of that."

With every new hero, art and game design intersected in important but often unpredictable ways. One need outweighed all others: making sure the characters were immediately identifiable in the middle of battle. Was their silhouette too similar to an existing character? Would their abilities and effects create too much visual complexity during gameplay? This need for readability formed the bedrock for the team's approach to designing heroes, but character art director Arnold Tsang posed the challenge a different way: "If you had to distill a hero down to the most basic elements, to describe who they are and what they do, can you do that visually?"

DOOMFIST

Doomfist launched on July 6, 2017, but he existed in the lore from the beginning. *Overwatch*'s announcement trailer featured Doomfist's gauntlet, a high-tech weapon locked in a museum display. The cinematic also referenced a battle between the character and a highly intelligent gorilla named Winston. These details stirred the imagination of *Overwatch*'s community, and a playable Doomfist became highly anticipated.

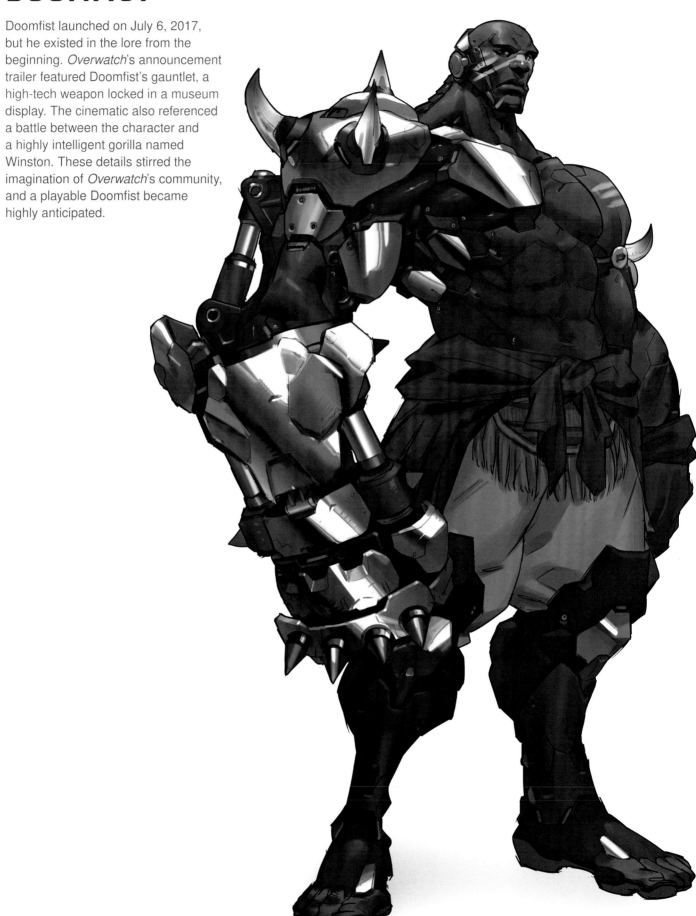

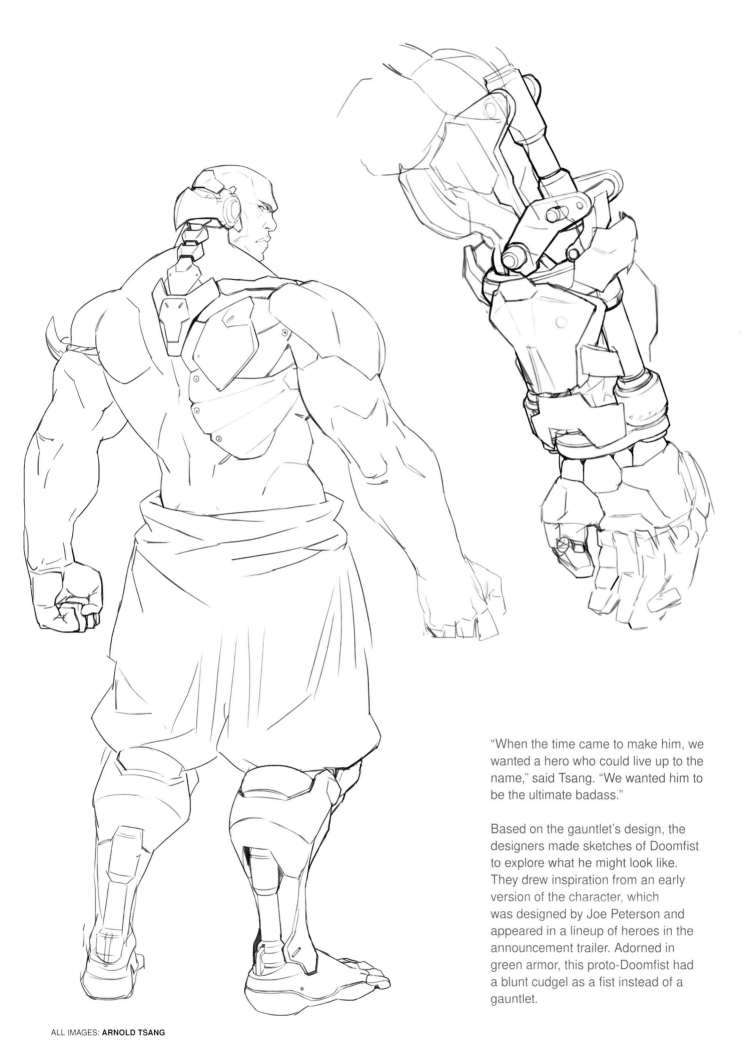

"When the time came to make him, we wanted a hero who could live up to the name," said Tsang. "We wanted him to be the ultimate badass."

Based on the gauntlet's design, the designers made sketches of Doomfist to explore what he might look like. They drew inspiration from an early version of the character, which was designed by Joe Peterson and appeared in a lineup of heroes in the announcement trailer. Adorned in green armor, this proto-Doomfist had a blunt cudgel as a fist instead of a gauntlet.

ALL IMAGES: **ARNOLD TSANG**

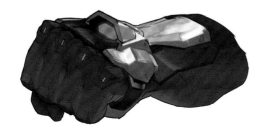

Later, the developers fleshed out more of his design. Heavily inspired by classic fighting games, they envisioned Doomfist as a pure melee character. "What would a character like that be in our game?" said lead hero designer Geoff Goodman. "When we started off, I made him a lot tankier so he could grab people. That didn't really work for a couple of reasons. One was that it was too strong if you could pick someone up and throw them in a pit next to you. I remember going back to the drawing board and thinking, 'Let's start over.' When making a hero, it helps to pick a single thing and rally around it. For him—if he's going to be Doomfist, if he's going to be punching people—we needed to come up with a super punch. He's got to have some ability where he can punch someone really hard. And what does that look like?" To achieve this goal, Goodman and the designers created a set of different melee attacks for Doomfist, including, as his ultimate ability, Meteor Strike.

ALL IMAGES: **ARNOLD TSANG**

Apart from these in-game abilities, the team also envisioned a backstory for Doomfist that revolved around his melee prowess. He grew up in Nigeria, where he mastered the martial art of Dambe. Through brute strength and unyielding determination, he fought his way to power and became a leading member of the international crime syndicate Talon.

"That was the first time we were doing a buff guy for *Overwatch*. It was a great opportunity to really push the anatomy. It was cool to explore that side and give us one point of reference for what a buff dude could look like in *Overwatch*," said the game's former lead character artist, Renaud Galand. "Up to that point, we knew how to stylize clothing, faces, hair, and mechanical parts, but we had not shown that much skin on a very muscular person."

MOVEMENT STUDY

Doomfist's physique, particularly his Dambe-inspired shirtless appearance, also influenced his animation style. Senior animator Kyongho Hong looked to the movements of real-life Dambe fighters as well as characters from classic fighting games to find stances and poses for Doomfist that would convey his aggressiveness, power, and agility.

One of the biggest challenges Hong faced with Doomfist was finding the right way to animate the hero's ranged attack. "His cannon on his left hand is tiny compared to his gauntlet," said Hong. "So even though we wanted to show off the gauntlet, we still wanted players to feel that his left-hand cannon was very dangerous. I made him tense his muscles when he is firing so people would feel that the weapon is very powerful and that the recoil is strong."

WEAPON IDEATION

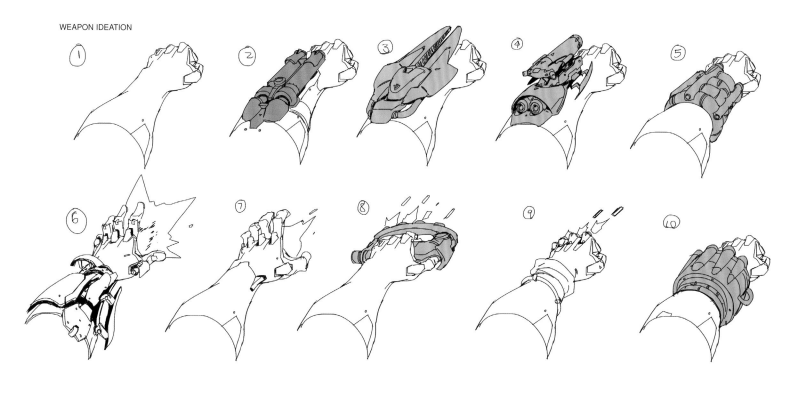

ABILITY IDEATION

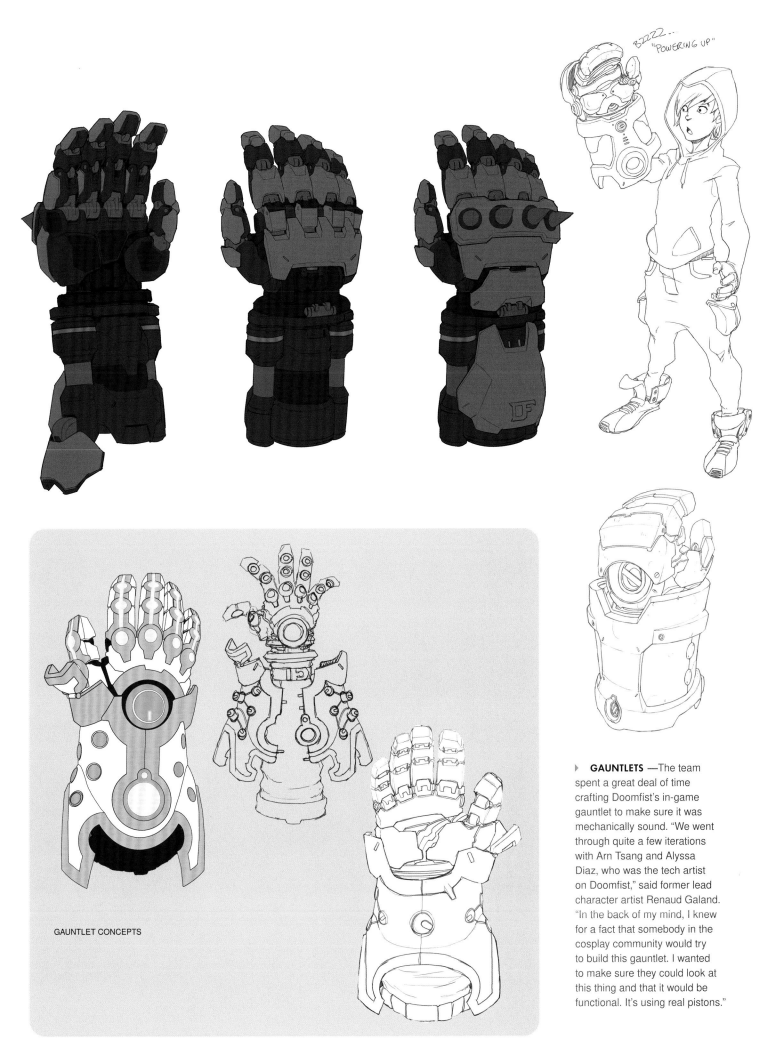

BZZZZ...
"POWERING UP"

GAUNTLET CONCEPTS

GAUNTLETS —The team spent a great deal of time crafting Doomfist's in-game gauntlet to make sure it was mechanically sound. "We went through quite a few iterations with Arn Tsang and Alyssa Diaz, who was the tech artist on Doomfist," said former lead character artist Renaud Galand. "In the back of my mind, I knew for a fact that somebody in the cosplay community would try to build this gauntlet. I wanted to make sure they could look at this thing and that it would be functional. It's using real pistons."

TOP: **ARNOLD TSANG**; BOTTOM & RIGHT: **CHRIS HA**

SKINS — When the designers work on new characters, ideas about new skins are always on their minds. Doomfist was no exception. The team created two unique skins to accompany his release, and both were designed to highlight different aspects of the hero's visual design and backstory.

"We don't design skins just for cosmetic purposes—they're not just something shiny," said former concept artist Ben Zhang. "We want something lore-driven, or something that is in line with their personality and what people love about the hero."

Doomfist's two launch skins drew from disparate aspects of the character. "How can we bring his traditions into the design?" said Tsang. "For the Spirit skin, we incorporated elements from African mythology—the idea of a godlike conqueror."

Conversely, for the Irin skin, the developers took the idea of Doomfist's cybernetic gauntlet and applied it to his entire body. This robotic version of the hero drew inspiration from characters found in popular comic and animation universes. "We also thought the metallic look would work great to highlight his physique," said Tsang.

IRIN

SPIRIT

ALL IMAGES: **ARNOLD TSANG**

SPRAYS — The developers always create a variety of sprays for each hero. Some of them touch on pop culture, movies, or popular memes that are related to the character. Some reference game mechanics. Others offer glimpses at a hero's past. Ultimately, all of the sprays help define who the hero is as a whole.

In the case of Doomfist, many of his sprays revolve around his melee prowess, while others tie into his backstory. Crater is a reference to the prison wall he punches through in his origin short. Wrapped depicts Doomfist as a young Dambe fighter, coiling rope around his fist in preparation for a fight.

ARNOLD TSANG, QIU FANG, ANH DANG, AND RYAN BENJAMIN

ORIGIN STORY For Doomfist, the developers took a different approach to his origin story than they had with most of the previous heroes. The character's dynamic movements and kinetic fighting style seemed like the perfect fit for 2-D animation. "You couldn't have picked a better character—he is very action-oriented," said Tsang. "Anime is great for super-snappy action—physical action. So this was the perfect medium for him. I love that we were able to get Genji and Tracer in there, too because those characters are also really dynamic."

The designers had previously experimented with 2-D animation in a limited way for Sombra's origin story in 2016. Based on the success of that piece, they took things even further with Doomfist. Partnering with Chinese animation house Wolf Smoke, the team crafted a bombastic origin story to introduce Doomfist to the world.

CHARACTER STUDIES

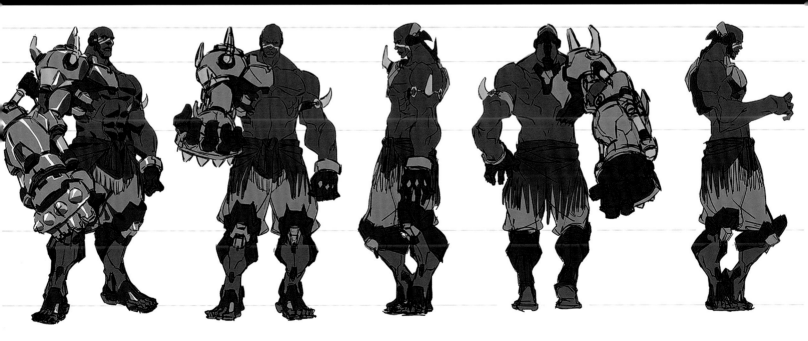

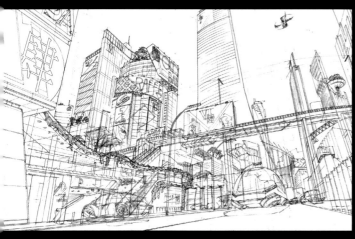

As with most of the origin pieces and cinematics, the details of Doomfist's story evolved over time through meetings and brainstorming sessions. "We get in these creative jam rooms and talk about what would be interesting," said director Doug Gregory. "We knew we needed a simple conceit, which was that Doomfist would have been in jail at some point." This idea led the team to stage part of the origin story in a prison—and have Doomfist smash through the wall with his bare hand. Through this extraordinary feat, the creators made a meaningful distinction between the character and his infamous weapon. "It was important to say he doesn't need the glove—he doesn't stop being Doomfist when he takes it off. He is whole without it."

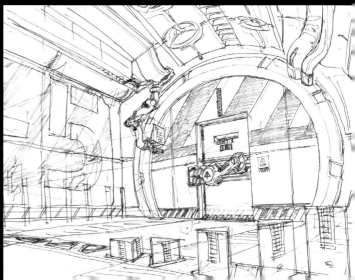

MOIRA

Heroes often go through drastic changes from early ideation to final design, and Moira is one such example. Released on November 3, 2017, the character was born from the team's desire to create an "evil" healer, which didn't exist in the lineup at that point. After discussing what the character's role would be in gameplay, the developers began fleshing out visual designs.

ALL IMAGES: **ARNOLD TSANG**

"We went back and looked at some sketches from Project Titan," said character art director Arnold Tsang, referring to the unreleased game that the team had worked on before *Overwatch*. "I really responded to the designs that were based around tentacles. Based on that, we came up with the first sketch."

This first sketch also incorporated elements Tsang and the team were intrigued by, such as making the hero feel androgynous, and heterochromia, a trait where someone has different-colored eyes. Ultimately, though, they were worried that this initial design wouldn't match the experience of playing the hero. She was meant to be a healer, but her tentacles gave the impression that she was a damage dealer.

CHARACTER IDEATION

ALL IMAGES: **ARNOLD TSANG**

"We went back to the drawing board," said Tsang. "We ended up with an ideation page of loose thumbnails."

The designers liked different elements from each of these ideation sketches, and they combined them into a new vision for the character. "For example, in the last sketch, we liked the idea of big sleeves that contain vials. One sleeve was healing, one sleeve did damage. That was intriguing," said Tsang. "We kept the look of the original sketch, but then changed other elements based on the new concepts, like the tubes instead of tentacles. We mashed it all together."

As work was being done on Moira's visual design, the developers were also discovering who she was. One of the lessons they had learned from their work on previous characters was the value of creating heroes who had relationships with existing heroes. They embraced this approach by giving Moira a strong connection to the crime syndicate Talon, as well as Blackwatch, the covert wing of the Overwatch organization.

ALL IMAGES: **ARNOLD TSANG**

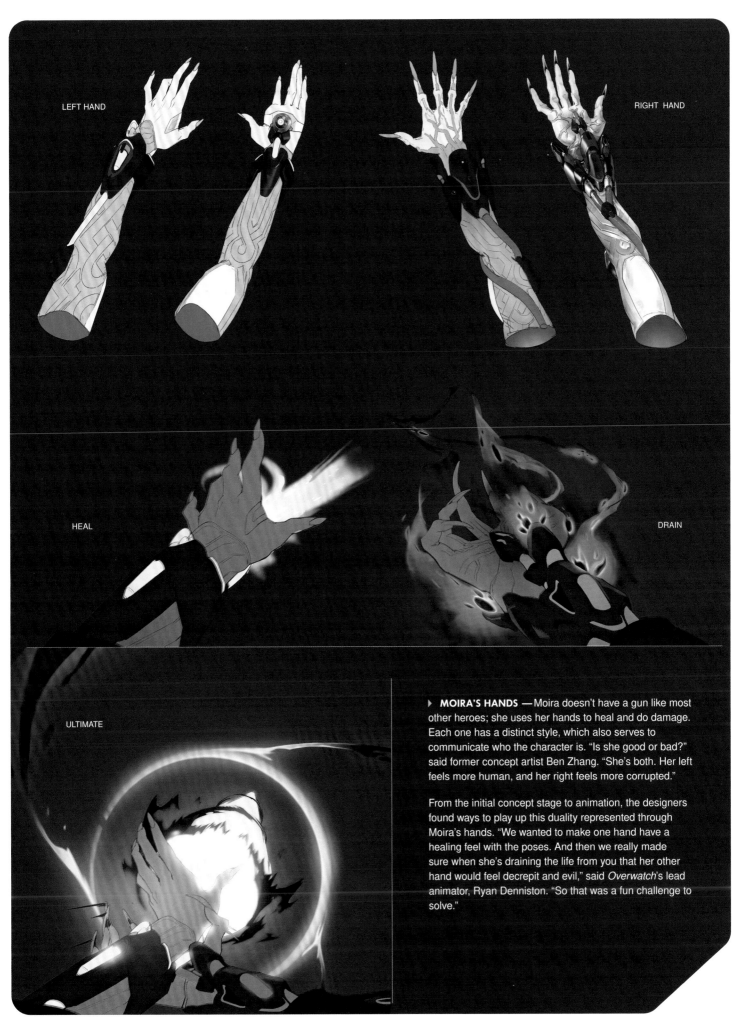

LEFT HAND

RIGHT HAND

HEAL

DRAIN

ULTIMATE

▶ **MOIRA'S HANDS** — Moira doesn't have a gun like most other heroes; she uses her hands to heal and do damage. Each one has a distinct style, which also serves to communicate who the character is. "Is she good or bad?" said former concept artist Ben Zhang. "She's both. Her left feels more human, and her right feels more corrupted."

From the initial concept stage to animation, the designers found ways to play up this duality represented through Moira's hands. "We wanted to make one hand have a healing feel with the poses. And then we really made sure when she's draining the life from you that her other hand would feel decrepit and evil," said *Overwatch*'s lead animator, Ryan Denniston. "So that was a fun challenge to solve."

ALL IMAGES: **BEN ZHANG**

▶ **VISUAL EFFECTS** —There are many components to creating a new hero, and one of them is concepting what a character's abilities and effects will look like. For Moira's healing ability, this proved to be more complicated than the designers had initially anticipated. "We had to convey something that is not light and not liquid either," said Zhang. "It was something in between. We had to make sure it wasn't completely physical. If I have two friendly players in front of me, I can heal the farther one—so the ability had to go through other people. It ended up being a combination of light and spray."

The team also created multiple concepts for Moira's ultimate ability to find a balance between something that would feel powerful but that wouldn't obstruct the player's vision. "The first one blocked too much of the screen," said Zhang. "We had to dial it back and iterate on things so it would work better in the game."

ULTIMATE BURST

ULTIMATE READY

ULTIMATE FIRING

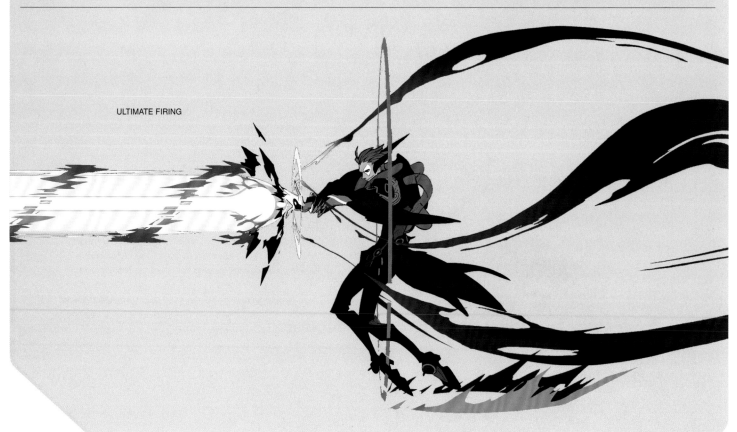

OASIS

SKINS — As with Doomfist, Moira's launch skins embraced different aspects of her character. Oasis relates to her backstory, when she worked as a geneticist in the highly advanced Iraqi city of Oasis. "The greatest scientists go there to pursue their research. Other countries might be too restrictive, but in Oasis the only limit is your own imagination," said Zhang, who designed the skin. The skin is an expression of the Oasis map: it incorporates that location's colors and style of technology. Scientific elements like double helixes also appear on Moira's armor and in the tubes that wrap around her shoulders.

ALL IMAGES: **BEN ZHANG**

GLAM

SPRAYS —For Moira's Nervous spray, the team drew on an element from her origin story. One of the early moments from the piece shows the character experimenting on a rabbit—and the animal depicted here is looking *very* uncomfortable in the hero's arms. Self-Experimentation takes this theme a step further by showing that Moira is willing to use herself as a test subject.

ANH DANG, ARNOLD TSANG, AND JANICE CHU

The origin story's other main goal was to expose Moira's ties to existing heroes and cement her importance in Overwatch history. The clearest example of this was the illustration showing her experimenting on Gabriel Reyes, confirming that she had a hand in transforming him into Reaper. "The character was intended to be gray, and it was fun seeing the different reactions to her. The way that Reyes looks when he sees shadowy smoke coming off him," said Chu. "The way that he's clearly welcoming to Moira when she's in Blackwatch, but Genji and McCree are less sure of her."

▶ **OUTFITS** — The origin story depicts Moira at different times of her life. Many of her origin story wardrobes were later released as skins. "At that point we had gotten smarter about planning out skins and finding opportunities to tease them," said Tsang. "We knew Moira was part of Talon and Blackwatch. She had a lot of history. How the outfits appeared in the origin story—we wanted them designed for the piece in anticipation that they would be translated into skins at some point."

NESSKAIN

BRIGITTE

"I always thought it would be interesting to do a tank-healer hybrid," said *Overwatch*'s lead hero designer, Geoff Goodman. "Internally, we called this gameplay concept the 'pally' because a paladin is already that kind of familiar archetype from other games. But what would a paladin look like in *Overwatch*? I was bringing up this idea, and [former lead writer] Michael Chu mentioned this character Brigitte. And it was sort of like, 'This is perfect. That could totally be her.' She wasn't built from the ground up to be that hero, but it worked really well."

Before her release as a playable hero on February 28, 2018, Brigitte appeared in different mediums outside the game. The *Dragon Slayer* comic introduced her as Reinhardt's apprentice, and the *Reflections* comic revealed she is Torbjörn's daughter. She was featured again in the "Honor and Glory" cinematic. These stories established her general appearance, as well as aspects of her backstory, concretely enough to begin working on Brigitte as a fully playable hero.

"We had a pretty good understanding of what she looked like, but when we started thinking about her actual design as a hero, there were still a lot of unanswered questions," said former concept artist Ben Zhang. "Being a character doing support, helping Reinhardt in battles, and now she has to actually fight side by side with him and be a reliable teammate. For that part of things we needed to see a design that pushed her more into that heroic role compared to the rest of the *Overwatch* characters."

ALL IMAGES: **BEN ZHANG**

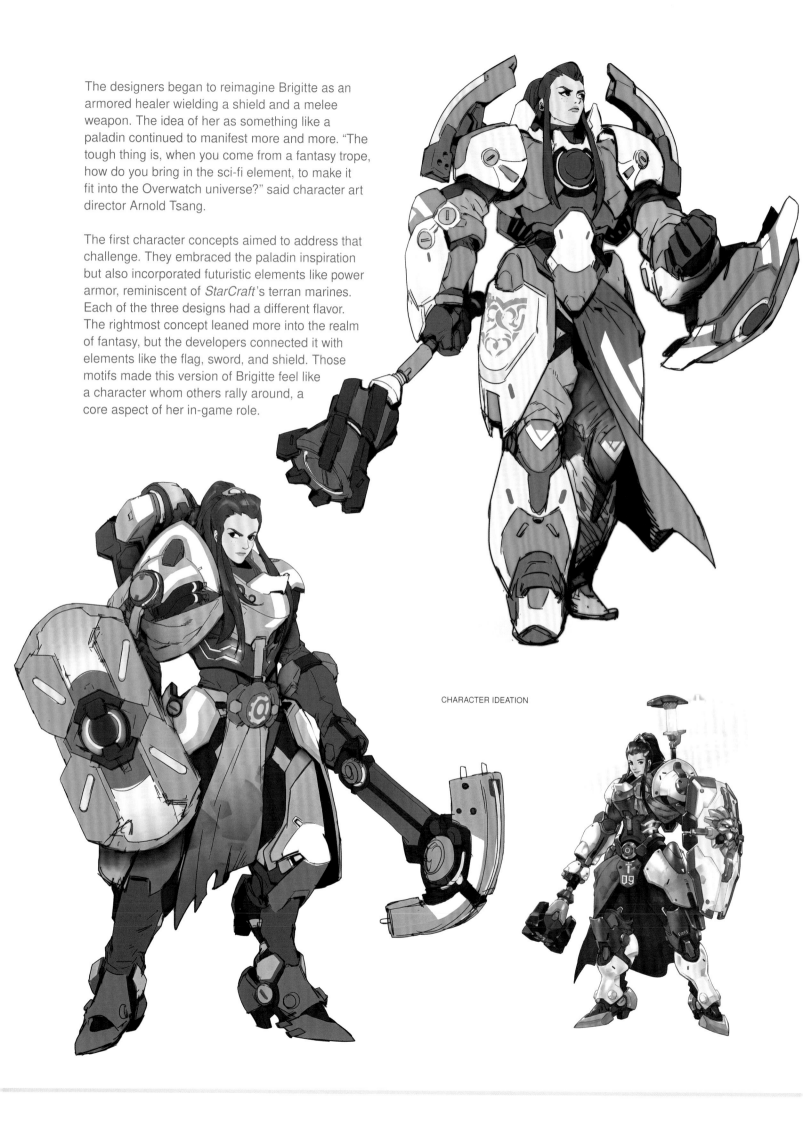

The designers began to reimagine Brigitte as an armored healer wielding a shield and a melee weapon. The idea of her as something like a paladin continued to manifest more and more. "The tough thing is, when you come from a fantasy trope, how do you bring in the sci-fi element, to make it fit into the Overwatch universe?" said character art director Arnold Tsang.

The first character concepts aimed to address that challenge. They embraced the paladin inspiration but also incorporated futuristic elements like power armor, reminiscent of *StarCraft*'s terran marines. Each of the three designs had a different flavor. The rightmost concept leaned more into the realm of fantasy, but the developers connected it with elements like the flag, sword, and shield. Those motifs made this version of Brigitte feel like a character whom others rally around, a core aspect of her in-game role.

CHARACTER IDEATION

"The second idea, I tried a weapon more like a flail or a hammer, because paladins do use those types of weapons. This is kind of a sci-fi version of it," said Zhang, who created the concepts. "But the character started to feel disengaging. The armor or the colors or some of the shape design started to feel too futuristic. When we design characters in *Overwatch*, we always want them to be relatable to the player."

The third concept tackled this relatability problem by grounding Brigitte in her engineering prowess. "She is the daughter of Torbjörn and also the squire for Reinhardt. It almost feels like she has two dads—both have a lot of impact on her and her choice to become an Overwatch member on the battlefield," said Zhang. "So then we talked about, maybe we should bring more Torbjörn tech influence into her. And at the same time, we can bring a little bit more knight-ish armor design from Reinhardt. So the ideas start to flow and come together."

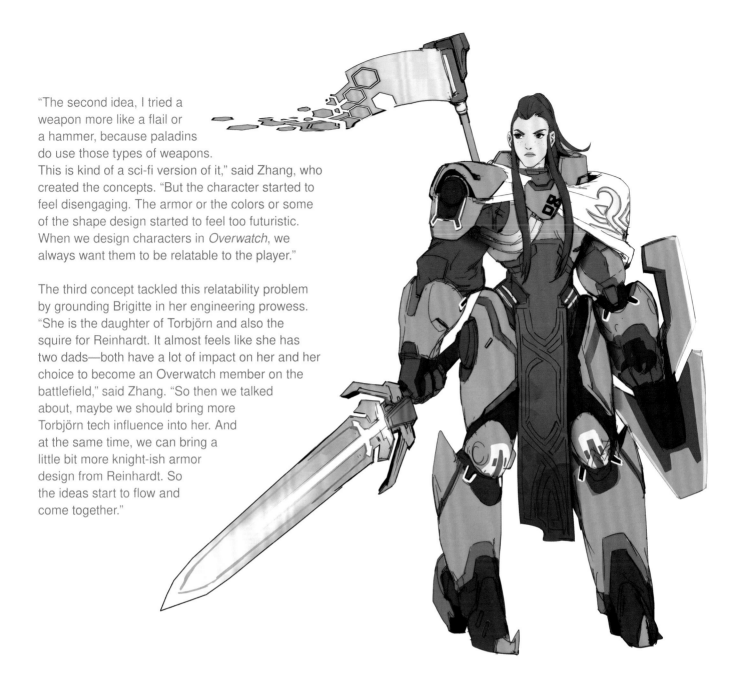

ALL IMAGES: **BEN ZHANG**

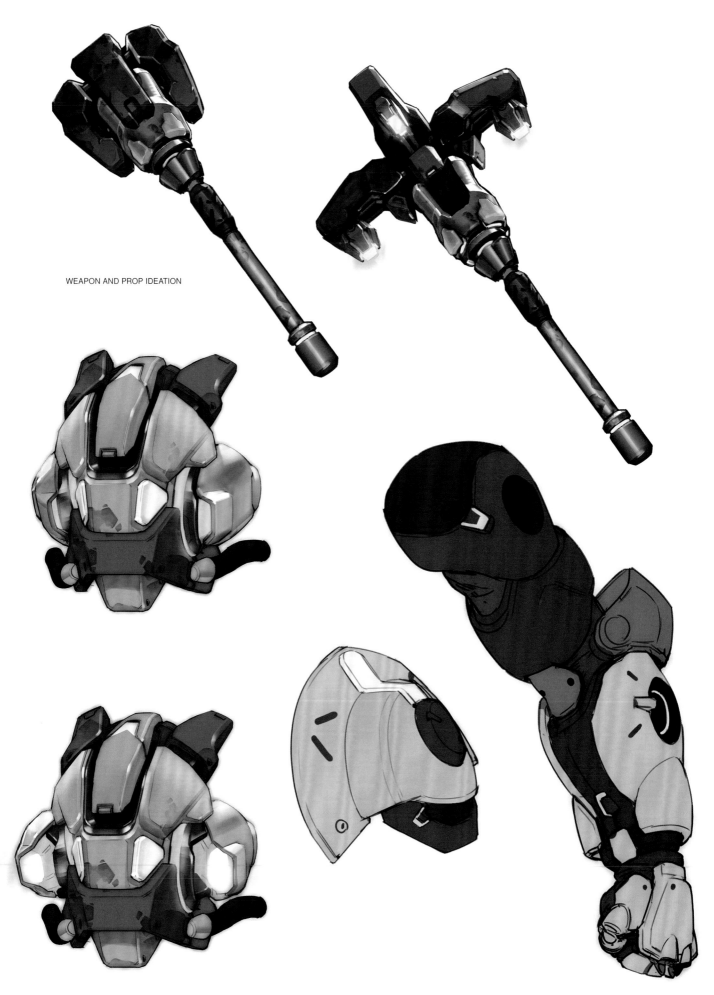

WEAPON AND PROP IDEATION

The developers connected to different parts of the three concepts, and these were combined into what would become Brigitte's final design. In the later stages of the art process, color also entered the conversation. "We wanted the color to be meaningful to telling the player who she was. At first, we had a version that was a little more red, closer to Torbjörn," said Zhang. "But you don't want it to just follow all the way to a point where she starts losing her identity, so we also looked at the color palette of the current hero lineup. The combination of stainless steel and painted yellow felt unique."

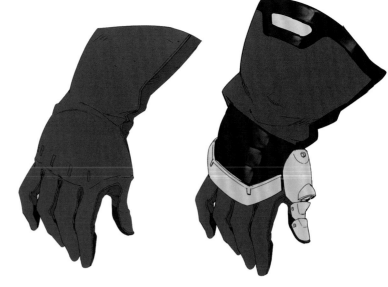

MOVEMENT STUDY

SKINS — When the team began brainstorming launch skins for Brigitte, two themes kept emerging: paladin and engineer. Both were deeply rooted in the hero's backstory and the original inspirations for her design. Concept artists David Kang and Ben Zhang reimagined Brigitte as if she existed in a medieval fantasy world with the Paladin skin. While detailing out her appearance, the developers looked for ways to hint at her role on the battlefield. The motif of a sun, emblazoned on her armor, tied into the fantasy trope of light as a source of healing.

SÓL

ENGINEER

For the Engineer skin, the developers wanted to create a look that felt like the prototype to Brigitte's current armor set—something she had forged in Torbjörn's workshop. Giving the outfit a work-in-progress look meant leaving more of the hero's body unarmored, which presented technical challenges. "From a rigging and silhouette point of view, you want to keep some stuff intact," said concept artist Morten Skaalvik. "For Brigitte, we wanted to avoid stripping off too much of the armor. Not only would this make certain animations not work, but it would also reduce her unique silhouette. We wanted to keep what's special about her in the skins."

"How color was used also played an important role in preserving Brigitte's uniqueness. "The color needs to feel different from the original—you want it to feel like a different fantasy than the original skin. I wanted people to look at this and think, 'Oh yeah, she's a mechanic.' So then what kind of colors does that represent?" said Skaalvik. "If you look at this character, her colors are dominant red with accents of green and yellow. I decided to do this to reference her father Torbjörn, the most iconic mechanic in Overwatch."

ALL IMAGES: **MORTEN SKAALVIK**

SPRAYS — "We use sprays as a way to push story elements or details about a character," said former concept artist Anh Dang. "Brigitte is a good example. She has a family photo. She's arm-wrestling, which shows she wants to be strong, but she's struggling compared to other characters.

The recurring motif of cats partly originated from an old character concept of a flying feline armed with a flamethrower. The team never added the hero, Jetpack Cat, to the game, but they found an opportunity to pay homage to it in Brigitte's origin story. The cinematic features an illustration of the young hero attaching armor to her pet cat. Felines also appear in other depictions of Brigitte's backstory, including a holiday family gathering in the *Reflections* comic.

QIU FANG, ANH DANG, AND JANICE CHU

ORIGIN STORY—Although Brigitte is undeniably influenced by her father, Torbjörn, and her mentor, Reinhardt, the team sought to use her origin story to clarify how she's different from them. The designers wanted to bring Brigitte out from the shadows of her larger-than-life influences, to show that she is her own fully formed character, with her own hopes, dreams, and view of the world.

"She's more like Torbjörn, but with a benevolent outlook. She's protecting other people. Not in the abstract sense . . . she literally wants to put the armor on and physically protect people," said *Overwatch*'s former lead writer, Michael Chu.

Compared to Brigitte's concept art, the illustrations featured in the origin story were an opportunity to show more of her personality. "Designing a character is all about the aesthetic, gear, and things like that," said Zhang, who created art for the origin short with Arnold Tsang. "But on the origin shorts, the purpose is more about telling a story. One part of that was showing the evolution of her armor set. She's building it in the workshop, welding it together and testing how it functions."

Many of the illustrations also focus on the idea of a mentor and a protégé, but the origin short ultimately reveals that Brigitte is more than just Reinhardt's apprentice. She is *his* guardian.

"The vibe of one shot—Brigitte bandaging Reinhardt—was originally inspired by an illustration Nesskain did," said Tsang. "It was so perfect."

Nesskain, who normally worked on the origin stories, was occupied with other projects during this period. But in his free time, he had created a number of illustrations depicting Reinhardt and Brigitte. "The origin story was very Nesskain-inspired," said Tsang. "I was glad I had something as brilliant as his work to draw from."

WRECKING BALL

On June 8, 2018, a new hero unlike any who had come before made his grand entrance into the world of Overwatch. Wrecking Ball is a weapon-laden mech piloted by a cuddly, highly intelligent hamster named Hammond.

When the idea of creating Wrecking Ball came up, the question on everyone's mind was whether it would fit in the Overwatch universe. Was it too quirky? Too absurd? The game already featured one intelligent animal—Winston—but Wrecking Ball seemed like an even further departure from reality.

ALL IMAGES: **ARNOLD TSANG**

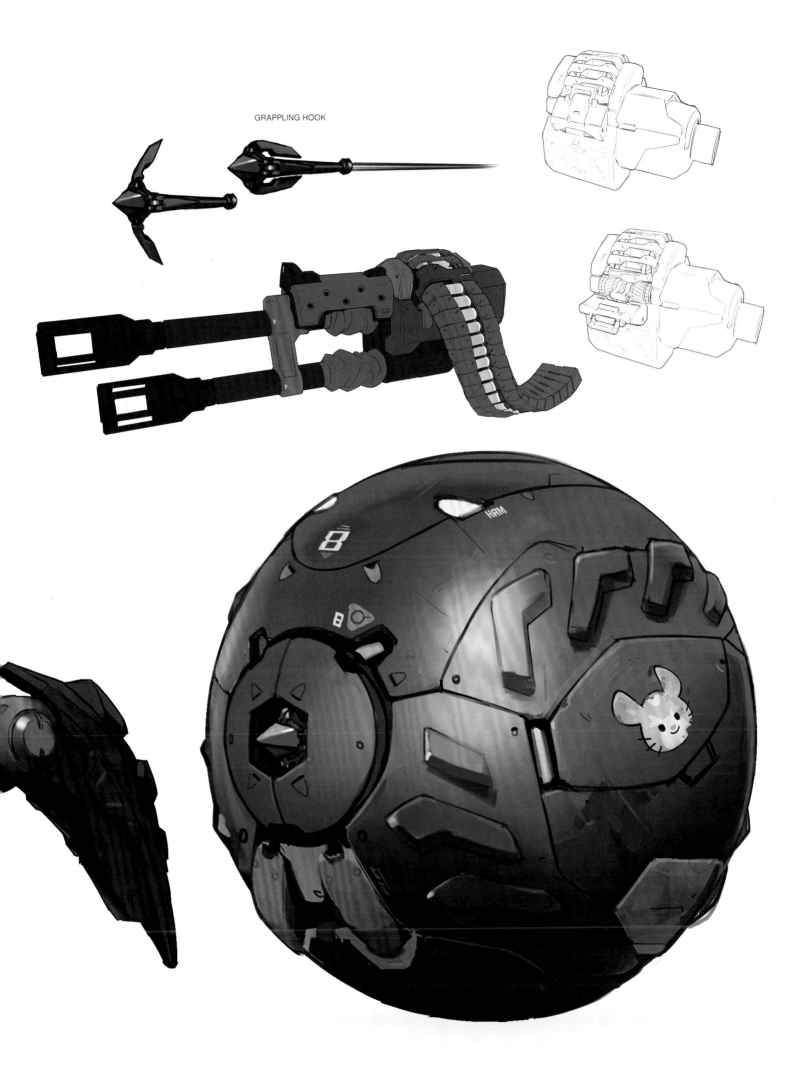

GRAPPLING HOOK

From a visual standpoint, concept art played a crucial role in determining whether Wrecking Ball could feel at home alongside the game's existing lineup of characters. The design originated from an old concept for a demolitionist hero. Some elements of this discarded character were incorporated into Junkrat, but the basic idea—a robot that could turn into a mechanized ball—became the foundation for Wrecking Ball.

From the outset, the issue was turning the character into a hero. "Initially, it felt more like a non-player character, since it didn't have a face," said character art director Arnold Tsang. "How can we make it more of a hero? It was kind of a joke at first, but we talked about the hamster in a ball idea."

EARLY MECH CONCEPT

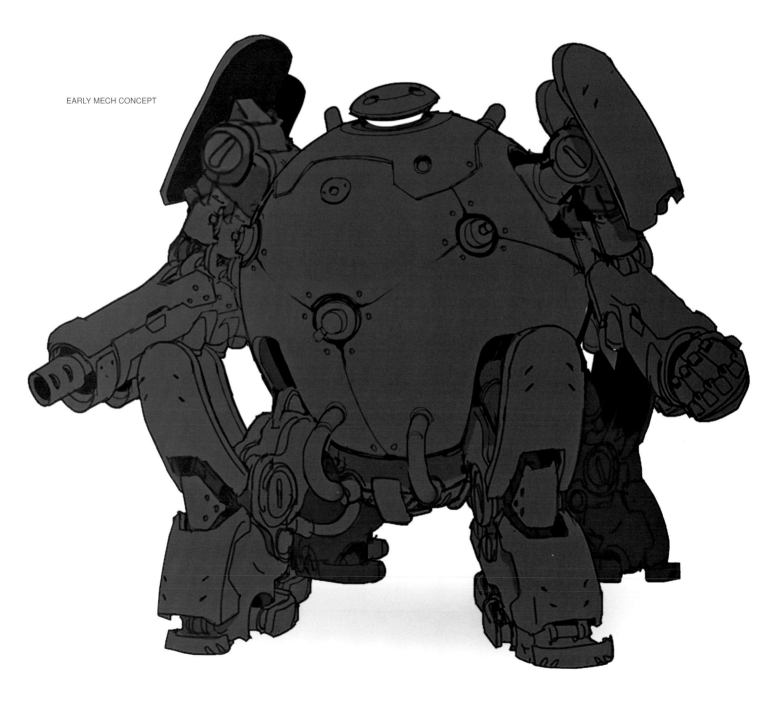

Through the concepting process, the hero evolved from a robotic hamster into a cute, furry one. The animal was larger than normal for the sake of readability—a real hamster would have been difficult to see in the game. "I put the concepts next to Tracer to see what could actually fit in the world," said Tsang. "The bottom row seemed to resonate the most with people."

Wrecking Ball's more whimsical nature allowed animators to do things that might not have fit the tone or style of other heroes in the game. "For most characters, once we develop their personality, there it is. You can't really break away from it or else you lose everything. That's the charm and appeal of the game," said lead animator Ryan Denniston. "We kind of pushed those rules with Wrecking Ball. Hammond has a huge personality. His hero select, his plays of the game, his emotes, his dance—his dance is amazing. It was a fun character to animate. It was kind of freeing in a way. We got to have fun with him and push the animation style."

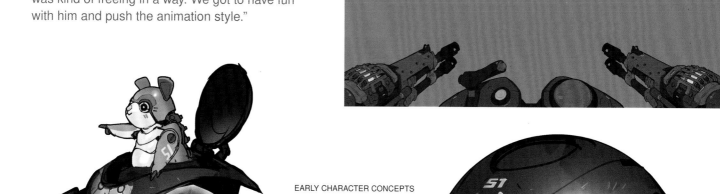

EARLY CHARACTER CONCEPTS

As is the case with every hero, when the team moved from the concepting stage to building the character in 3-D, certain aspects of the design changed. The developers had never done stylized animals at Wrecking Ball's scale, and they made structural changes to the snout and other areas of the face.

Introducing Wrecking Ball to the lineup was certainly a risk, but in the end, designers had crafted a hero who worked as a part of the Overwatch universe *and* was fun to play. But most importantly, it opened the door for pushing the design envelope even further.

ALL IMAGES: **ARNOLD TSANG**

SPRAYS —The 8 spray is a subtle reference to Wrecking Ball's backstory. During his time on the Horizon Lunar Colony, he wore a jumpsuit denoting him as "Specimen 8." This number briefly appears in Wrecking Ball's origin story.

ANH DANG, ARNOLD TSANG, AND **QIU FANG**

HORIZON

HAM08
HRZN

MAYHEM

HAM

ALL IMAGES: **DAVID KANG**

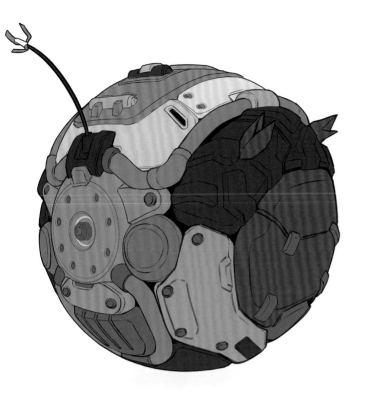

SKINS — Wrecking Ball's Horizon skin reflected an important part of the hero's backstory. Originally a test subject on the moon's Horizon Lunar Colony, the hamster fled to Earth aboard an escape pod. The designers imagined that this vehicle was still the core of the mech, but Hammond had gradually covered it in other pieces of metal.

The Junker skin focused on another period of Hammond's history. After arriving on Earth, he found a home among the scrapyards of Junkertown. This mech was built from the materials he scavenged from his surroundings.

"Hammond being an animal, what is the difference between him and other animals in *Overwatch*? He needs to adapt to his environment," said Zhang. "We tried to blend the mech with the design of the Junkertown map."

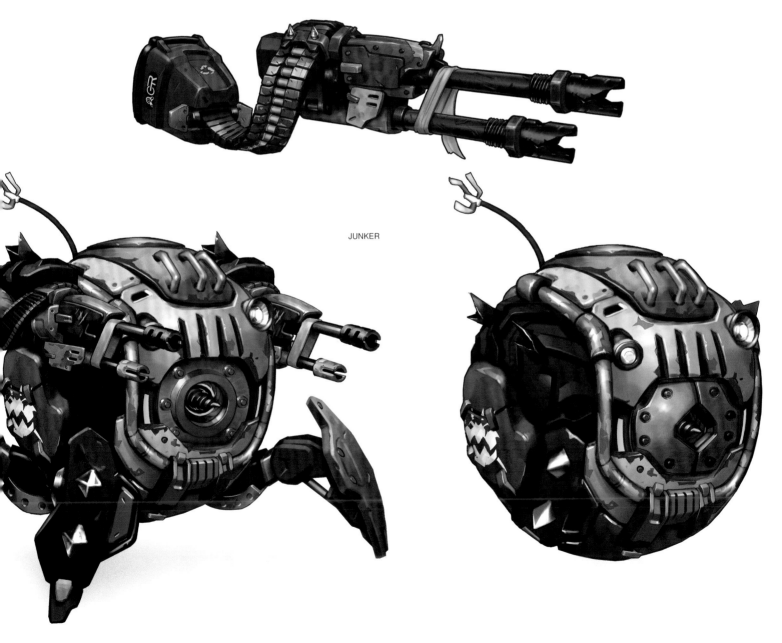

JUNKER

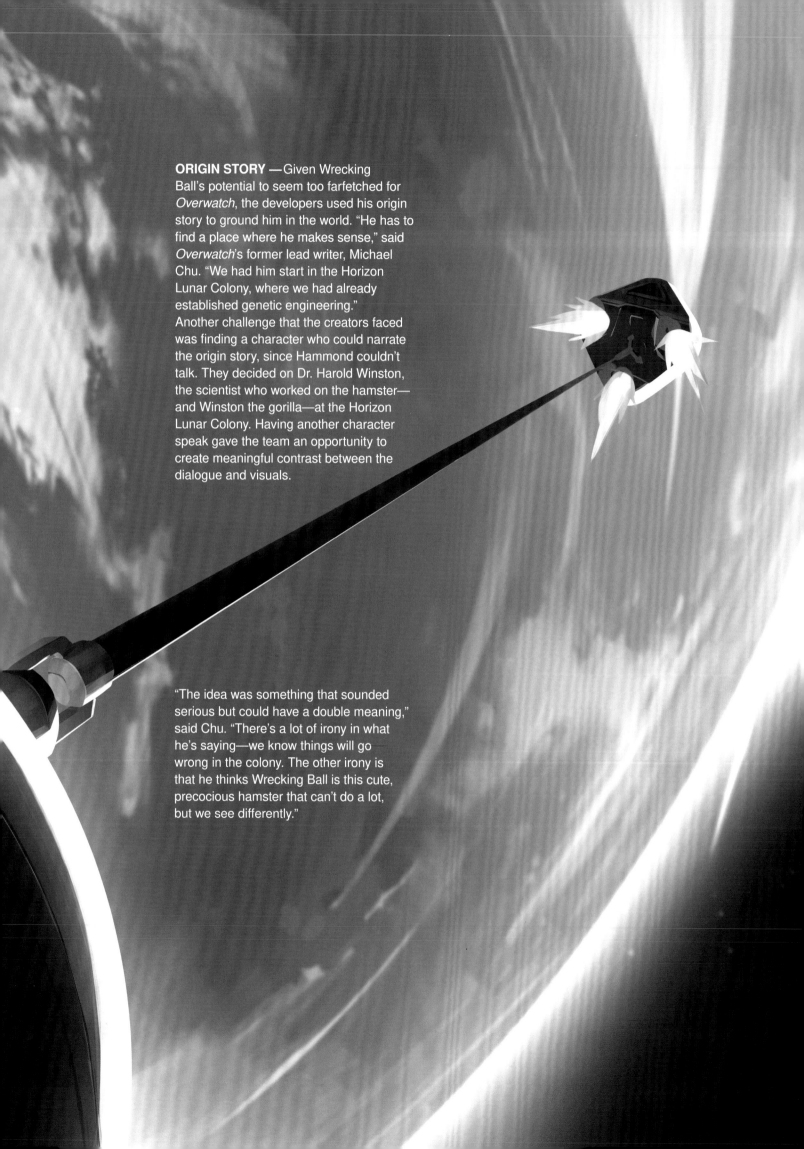

ORIGIN STORY —Given Wrecking Ball's potential to seem too farfetched for *Overwatch*, the developers used his origin story to ground him in the world. "He has to find a place where he makes sense," said *Overwatch*'s former lead writer, Michael Chu. "We had him start in the Horizon Lunar Colony, where we had already established genetic engineering." Another challenge that the creators faced was finding a character who could narrate the origin story, since Hammond couldn't talk. They decided on Dr. Harold Winston, the scientist who worked on the hamster—and Winston the gorilla—at the Horizon Lunar Colony. Having another character speak gave the team an opportunity to create meaningful contrast between the dialogue and visuals.

"The idea was something that sounded serious but could have a double meaning," said Chu. "There's a lot of irony in what he's saying—we know things will go wrong in the colony. The other irony is that he thinks Wrecking Ball is this cute, precocious hamster that can't do a lot, but we see differently."

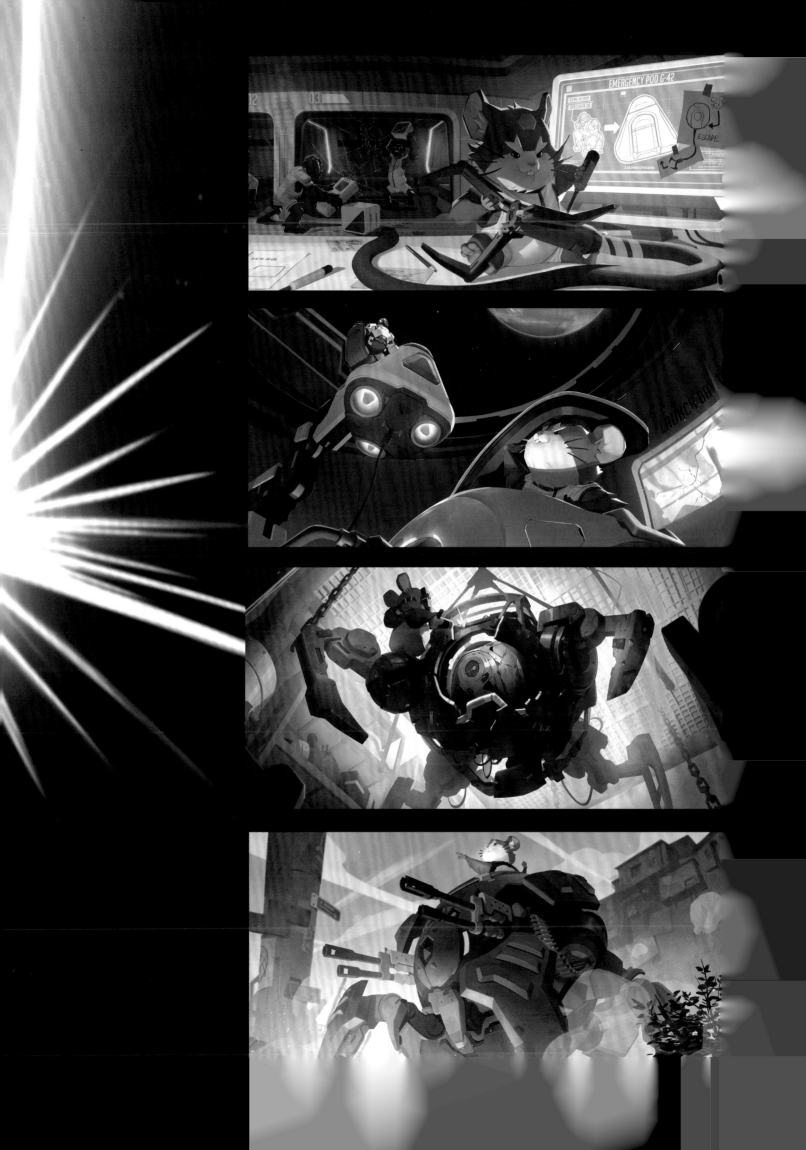

ASHE

Ashe's journey to becoming a playable character was different from most other heroes. She originated from the "Reunion" cinematic, a story that revolved around a confrontation between McCree and his former allies in the Deadlock Gang.

CHARACTER
IDEATION

TATTOO

The filmmakers created Ashe as the gang's strong-willed and memorable leader—someone with the grit to go toe to toe with McCree. The moment everyone saw the first concepts, they loved her. "We treated her like we would if she was going to be a hero," said character art director Arnold Tsang. "After seeing an early version of the cinematic, lead hero designer Geoff Goodman even started thinking about her abilities." But before Ashe would make it into the game on November 2, 2018, the team had to iterate on her look. The hero's initial concepts, created by visual development artist Jungah Lee, drew inspiration from bikers, cowboys, and vampire hunters. The question for the designers was which one of those concepts to focus on.

CHARACTER AND
WEAPON IDEATION

"The pale skin and white hair felt too vampiric. The cowboy thing was more for McCree. So we went more toward the biker with a little touch of a western vibe," said Tsang.

As things like the leather jacket, shirt, and tie crept into the concepts, Ashe started coming into her own. She exuded class and style with a menacing edge, which set her apart from McCree and the other members of the Deadlock Gang. Additional elements, such as the tech incorporated onto her arm, grounded her in *Overwatch*'s futuristic world.

TOP: **JUNGAH LEE**; BOTTOM: **BEN ZHANG**

And then there was B.O.B., Ashe's trusted sidekick.

"After we saw that early version of the 'Reunion' cinematic, I started to whip up a quick paper design of Ashe, but former designer Adrian Finol also did it too," said *Overwatch*'s lead hero designer, Geoff Goodman. "We both had the same instinct. We were comparing notes, and we both picked B.O.B. as the ultimate."

MOVEMENT STUDY

1.

2.

3.

4.

TOP: **JUNGAH LEE**; BOTTOM: **BEN ZHANG**

Everyone was enamored by the idea of a burly, mustached omnic in a bowler hat. The designers liked the initial idea so much that little changed between the first concept and the final design. The challenge with B.O.B. was actually incorporating him into the game.

"In playtesting he was a lot of fun, but there were a lot of challenges trying to create another character. There are a lot of memory, texture, and server considerations we're working with. It's always difficult as we start to push those boundaries," said Goodman. "There was a lot of concern, especially with B.O.B. being as big as he is. Can we have them both look good while essentially having to fit them within the resource limitations of a single character model? Honestly, he almost got cut. It got to a point where we thought we couldn't do it. But then the artists and the engineers really stepped up and got things done. Luckily, Ashe and B.O.B. both look great in the game."

EARLY CHARACTER CONCEPTS

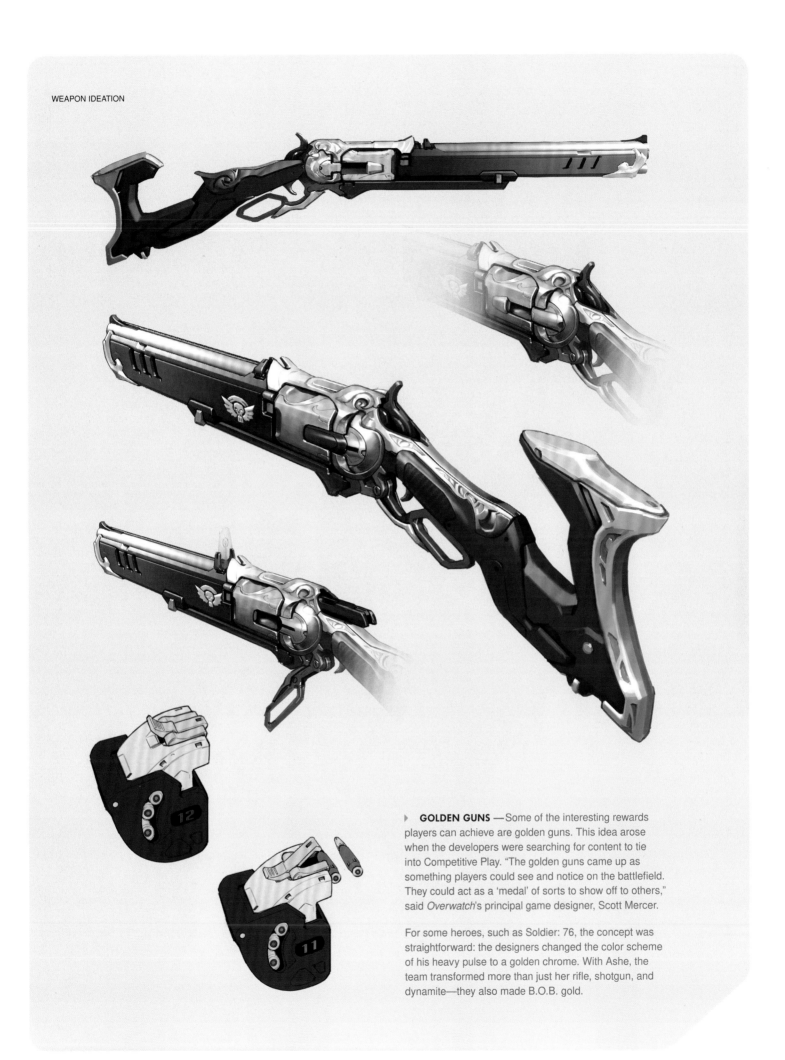

▶ **GOLDEN GUNS —** Some of the interesting rewards players can achieve are golden guns. This idea arose when the developers were searching for content to tie into Competitive Play. "The golden guns came up as something players could see and notice on the battlefield. They could act as a 'medal' of sorts to show off to others," said *Overwatch*'s principal game designer, Scott Mercer.

For some heroes, such as Soldier: 76, the concept was straightforward: the designers changed the color scheme of his heavy pulse to a golden chrome. With Ashe, the team transformed more than just her rifle, shotgun, and dynamite—they also made B.O.B. gold.

ALL IMAGES: **BEN ZHANG**

SKINS —The decision to make B.O.B. a part of Ashe's in-game abilities meant that any skin created for the hero would have to account for the omnic too—and that opened the door to many creative opportunities. "Ashe is really fun for concept artists to work on because of B.O.B.," said Tsang. "You can't always fit all the visual elements you want on a character. But with Ashe, you can include some of them on B.O.B. instead."

The two skins released with Ashe at launch were Mobster and Safari, both of which

EPIC SKINS

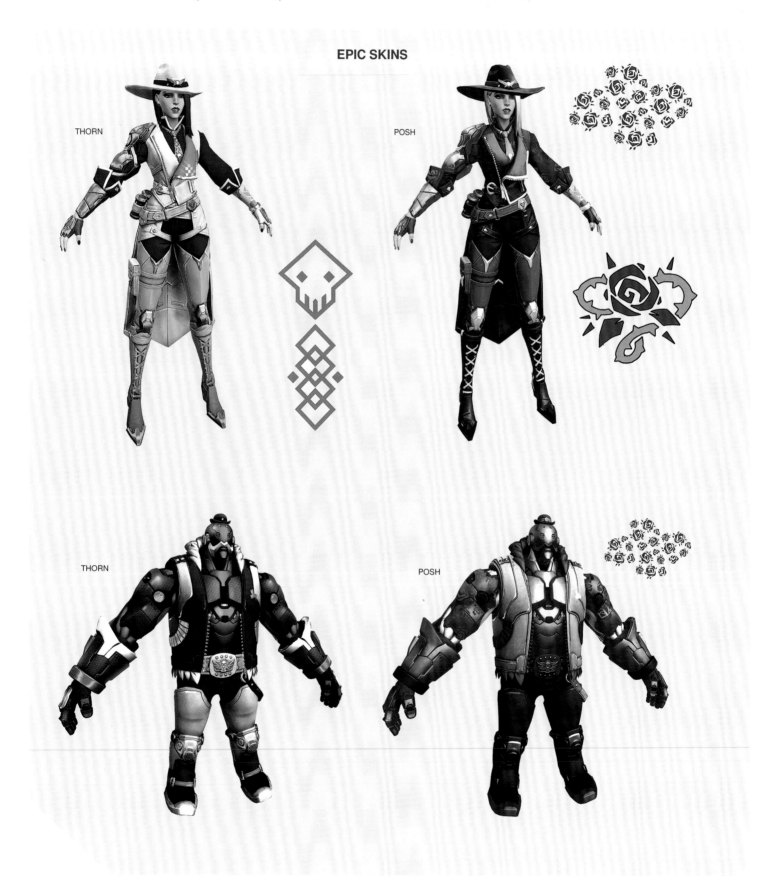

THORN

POSH

THORN

POSH

tie into some of the hero's thematic elements. "The most fun thing is finding a way to see the character in a different light that still relates to how they look. Ashe is a cowboy with a sidekick, and I'm trying to think about different ways to look at that," said concept artist Morten Skaalvik, who created the skins. "She's a vigilante—what other vigilantes can I relate that to? You want everyone's skin to be recognizable right away, like, *Oh, this is Mobster Ashe.*"

ALL IMAGES: **MORTEN SKAALVIK**

For all of Ashe's skins, the designers identify the unique traits both characters have, then play with them to fit the theme of the skin. B.O.B.'s mustache, for example—"I wanted to keep it, as it's such a big part of his personality, but change it, so it fits the theme of the skin I'm going for," said Skaalvik. "That's also how we work with riggers and 3-D modelers. What can we change and what can we not change about the character?"

Every character has iconic animations that are based on parts of their original skins, and that means certain elements from their design can't be changed. "A great example is McCree's hat. Because we have a very iconic animation where he's literally touching the brim of his hat, we lock down the shape of that brim forever," said former lead character artist Renaud Galand. "So you can change the way it looks, but you can't remove it."

SAFARI

SPRAYS —The developers embraced the relationship between Ashe and B.O.B. for many of the hero's sprays. Back to Back, Getaway, and Exchange all revolve around the pair's heist activities; Butler references their past, when B.O.B. was part of Ashe's life before she became an outlaw. The Teatime spray is a melding of the two ideas—it shows that even in their current life of crime, B.O.B. still waits on Ashe, and she still enjoys the finer things in life.

ALL IMAGES: **AQUATIC MOON**

While the designers were experimenting with Baptiste's abilities and gameplay style, they were also brainstorming what the hero looked like. "We wanted him to be handsome," said former concept artist Ben Zhang. "But before the handsome factor came into play, he used to be a lot younger and pretty agile."

Early concept art portrayed Baptiste as a combat medic who could quickly traverse the battlefield.

Gradually, as the designers fleshed out more of the character's backstory, they aged up Baptiste and gave him a bodybuilder physique. This affected how animators approached the hero as well. "Getting him to feel heavy and clarifying his movement style took a few iterations to get right," said lead animator Ryan Denniston. "He stomps down. If you watch his run-cycle, he has an extra-heavy hit when he lands."

MOVEMENT STUDY

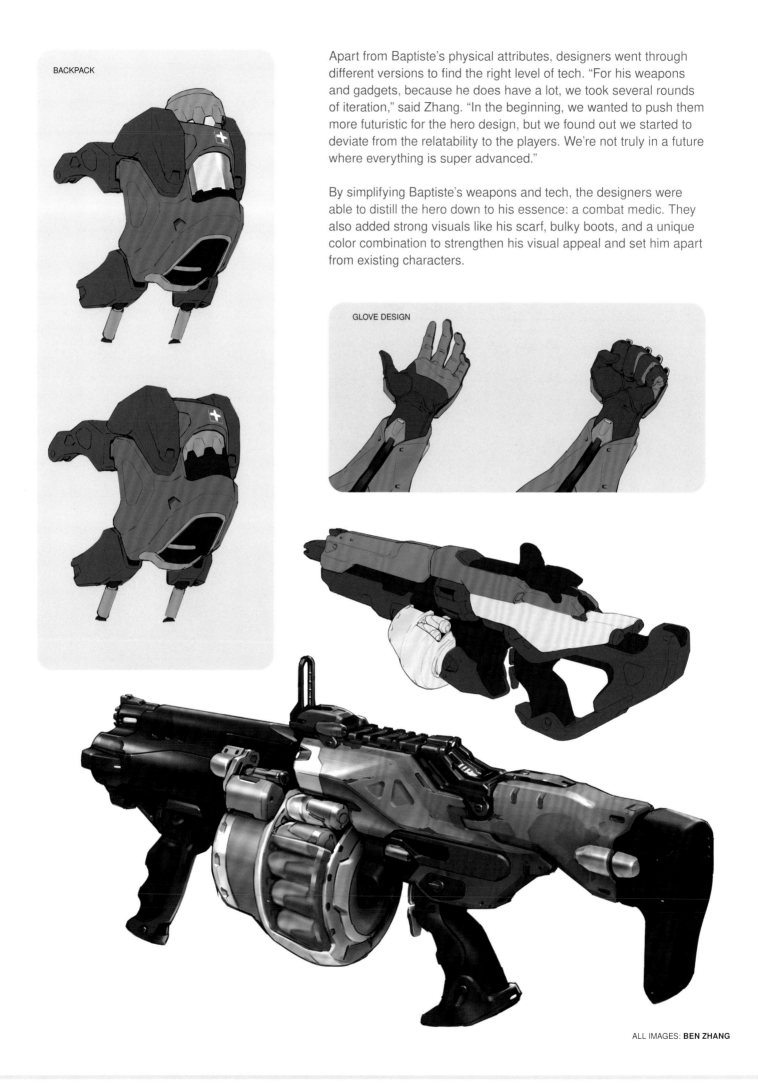

BACKPACK

Apart from Baptiste's physical attributes, designers went through different versions to find the right level of tech. "For his weapons and gadgets, because he does have a lot, we took several rounds of iteration," said Zhang. "In the beginning, we wanted to push them more futuristic for the hero design, but we found out we started to deviate from the relatability to the players. We're not truly in a future where everything is super advanced."

By simplifying Baptiste's weapons and tech, the designers were able to distill the hero down to his essence: a combat medic. They also added strong visuals like his scarf, bulky boots, and a unique color combination to strengthen his visual appeal and set him apart from existing characters.

GLOVE DESIGN

ALL IMAGES: **BEN ZHANG**

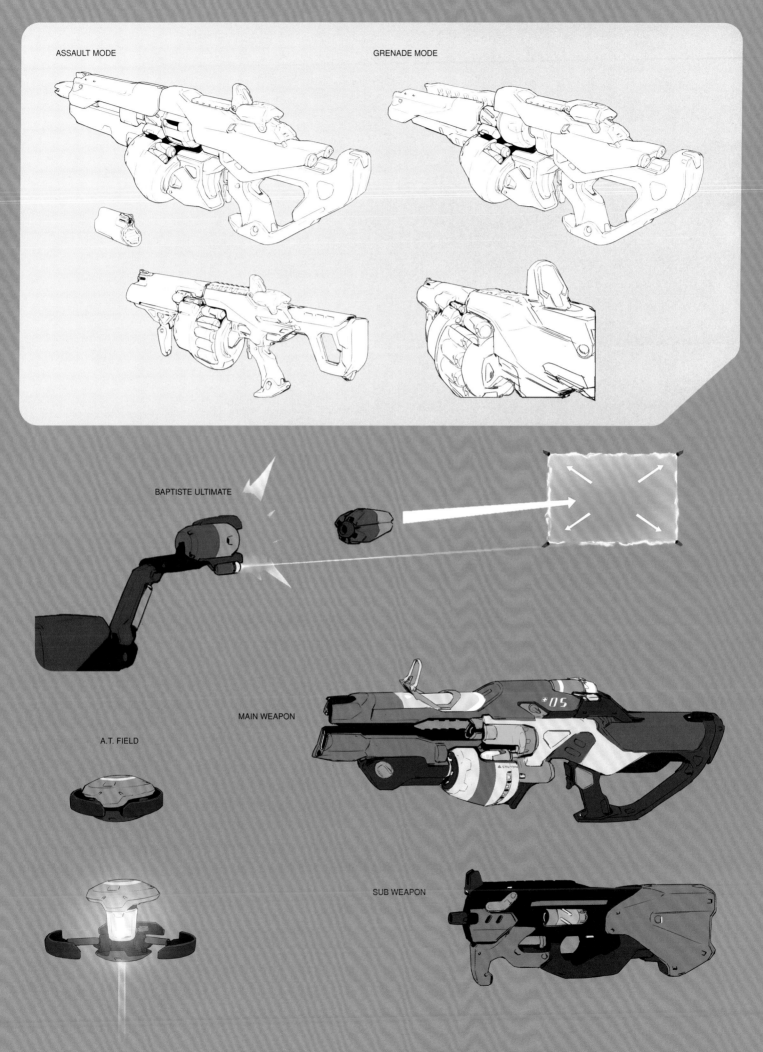

ASSAULT MODE

GRENADE MODE

BAPTISTE ULTIMATE

A.T. FIELD

MAIN WEAPON

SUB WEAPON

SKINS — Baptiste's skins were inspired by his home country and his history. Because Baptiste had spent time as part of an elite military team, Zhang and the developers crafted the Spec Ops skin. It played into the fantasy of the hero as a support specialist and tactician. The octopus logo was designed to represent Baptiste's former military group—the Caribbean Coalition's special ops. Baptiste's Buccaneer skin drew on his Caribbean roots in a more stylized way. "We had done a lot of pirate skins at that point already, but because that genre is so rich in visual language, it wasn't too hard to find unique areas to explore," said Tsang, who worked on the skin. "Because of Baptiste's heroic nature, we wanted him to feel more like one of the high-ranking pirates on the ship—he has a lot of gold on, and he wears a cool jacket." Tsang and the designers also applied pirate themes to specific elements on Baptiste's original design. They transformed his high-tech eyepiece into an eyepatch, and they replaced the antenna on his backpack with a cutlass.

SPEC OPS

BUCCANEER

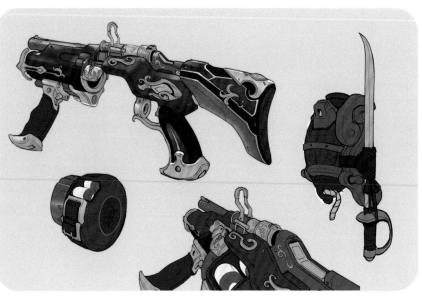

TOP: **ARNOLD TSANG**; BOTTOM: **ANH DANG**

SPRAYS —When approaching sprays, the team would often brainstorm small details that wouldn't normally be shown in the game or cinematics: what a character's favorite food is, what types of books he or she enjoys reading, and other more personal features. From those discussions, the designers incorporated little clues about who the heroes are as people into the sprays. Baptiste received a spray with a tropical drink.

"Maybe a fruity drink is his thing. He likes to kick back and have a cocktail," said former concept artist Anh Dang, who created some of Baptiste's sprays. "With newer characters, we focused less on graphic logos and way more on character-focused sprays. Either them portraying different emotions, or stuff that was important to them, or details about their life."

ARNOLD TSANG, ANH DANG, NESSKAIN, AND BEN ZHANG

NESSKAIN

ORIGIN STORY — Baptiste's origin story is tragic. He grew up in the shadow of the Omnic Crisis, a horrific conflict between omnics and humans that claimed millions of innocent lives. "This was a rare opportunity to show a character who was growing up during that—the first chance to see and provoke the idea in people's heads," said *Overwatch*'s former lead writer, Michael Chu. "Even though we talk about the Omnic Crisis as a great victory, the reality of living through it wasn't that great."

Baptiste survived the Omnic Crisis, but it set him on a winding path through good and evil. Each of the origin story's illustrations depicts another step along that road—another choice Baptiste made. For the images, artist Nesskain chose colors that would evoke an emotion or feeling relating to that period of the hero's life.

"The first image, when you see young Baptiste—I wanted it to feel dusty and gray, but I also gave it a little bit of warmth from the things burning around

him," said Nesskain. "The illustration where he's joining Talon is red—director Jeramiah Johnson wanted it to feel like that choice was a bad idea, and it had to seem dangerous."

Many of the shots in the origin piece begin with a close-up on a character and then slowly zoom out to reveal the background, or vice versa. This technique presented a challenge for Nesskain—it meant he had to create large and richly detailed illustrations for every scene in the cinematic.

But the use of close-ups was critical to making a connection between viewers and Baptiste.

"In that opening shot, we wanted you to feel like you were in the firefight with Baptiste. You're not necessarily seeing the whole battlefield yet, but you see him," said the piece's director, Jeramiah Johnson. "We wanted to put you in his place and make the audience feel like they were with him in those moments."

SIGMA

Following the release of Baptiste, the designers explored the idea of an "evil" tank. They imagined that the character would share some gameplay mechanics with Reinhardt—someone who could create barriers and attack from midrange. Based on these ideas, concept art was created for a burly, boisterous Samoan character named Mauga. The team was very excited about the design, but there was one major issue.

"Mauga looks like a character who wants to jump into the fight. We tried to make it work. We had him punch out barriers and made everything physical," said character art director Arnold Tsang. "But once we realized the art and design didn't match, we had to hit the reset button. It was a huge lesson for us— we learned to make decisions earlier."

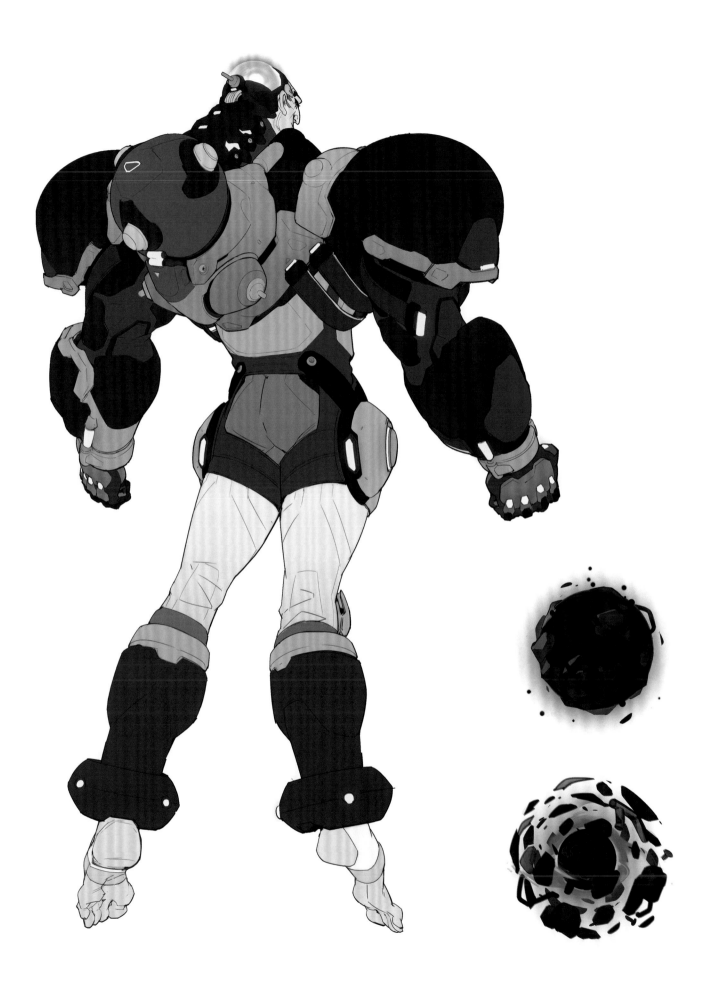

ALL IMAGES: **QIU FANG**

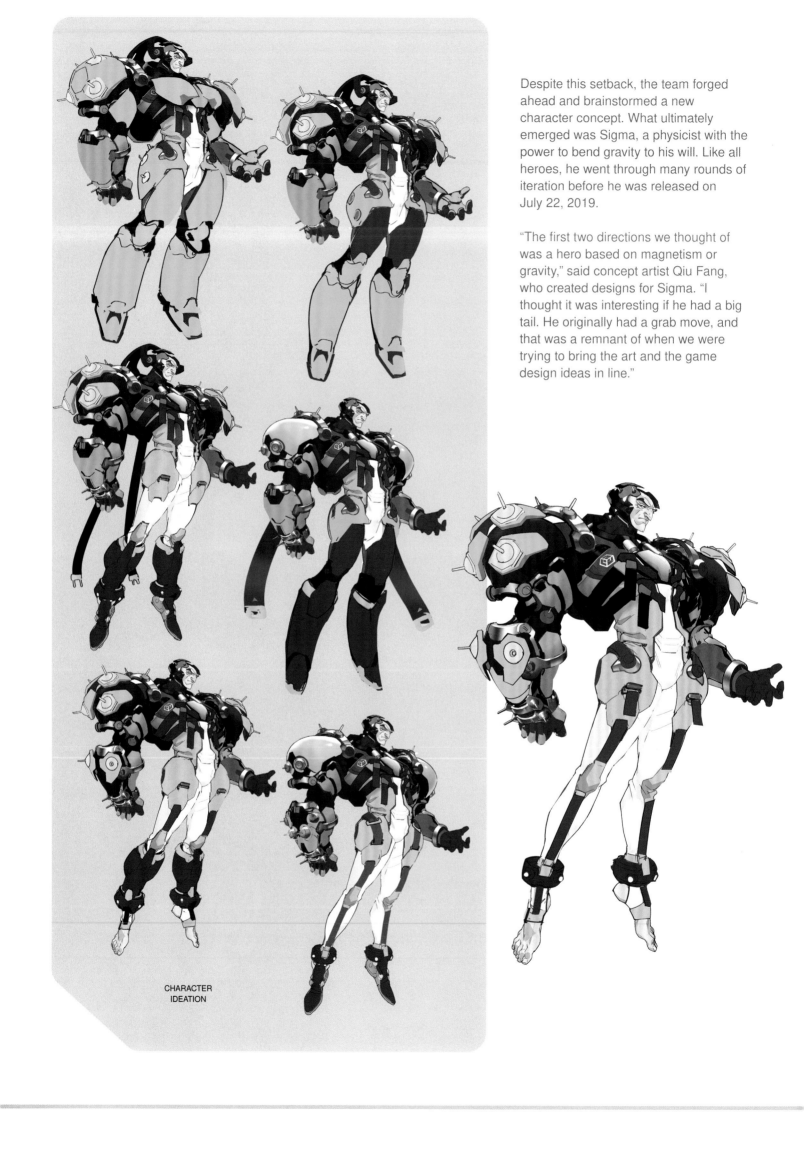

Despite this setback, the team forged ahead and brainstormed a new character concept. What ultimately emerged was Sigma, a physicist with the power to bend gravity to his will. Like all heroes, he went through many rounds of iteration before he was released on July 22, 2019.

"The first two directions we thought of was a hero based on magnetism or gravity," said concept artist Qiu Fang, who created designs for Sigma. "I thought it was interesting if he had a big tail. He originally had a grab move, and that was a remnant of when we were trying to bring the art and the game design ideas in line."

CHARACTER
IDEATION

EARLY CHARACTER
CONCEPTS

ALL IMAGES: **QIU FANG**

Ultimately, the team went away from the "grab" ability, and Sigma's physique also underwent drastic changes. The original idea for the design was that he would be a muscular character, but Fang explored a different path. "With a tank, there are certain things you can't get away from, like a big silhouette and bulky proportions," he said. "I wanted a tall, thinner character who felt like he used his powers—instead of his physique—to be a tank. A lot of the balance was how thin he can get."

Fang and the team explored different amounts of armor for Sigma to find the right look for him—something that felt appropriate for a tank but was also different from other characters. As more clothing and metal were added to the hero, a new concern arose that he might look too much like a robot or a cyborg.

One way Fang and the developers brought the humanity back to Sigma was through his feet. "He originally had shoes. Then people started talking about him not having any," said Fang. "He also didn't have a lot of skin showing, and showing the skin on his feet made him a lot more unique. It ended up helping me solidify the character."

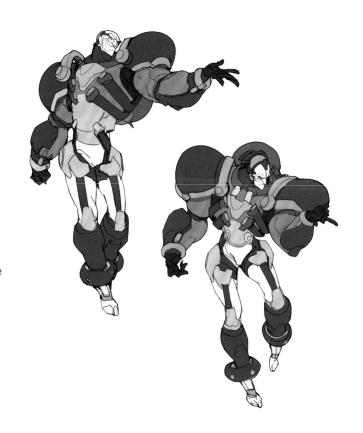

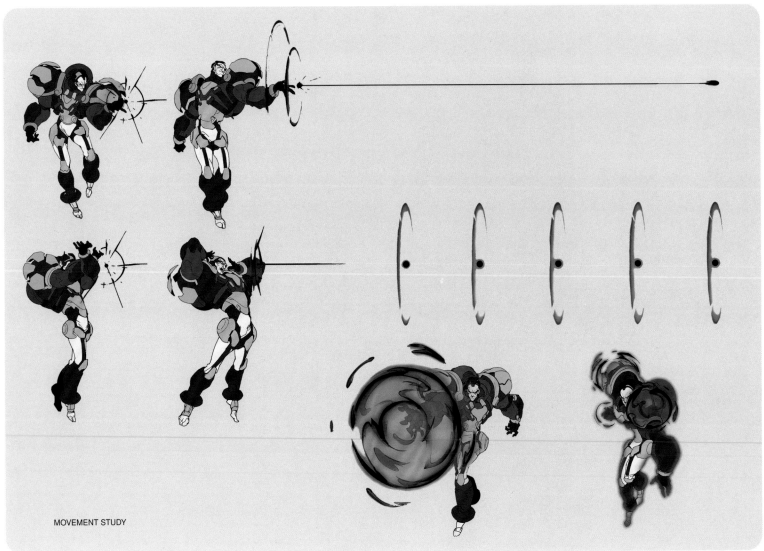

MOVEMENT STUDY

PROPHET

ORACLE

SKINS — Sigma's Prophet skin was inspired by the hero's disassociation with time and reality. "This one was fun. I like this type of theme in general—it's kind of magical," said Fang, who created the skin. "And I thought it fit Sigma well since he's this psychic-type character. He's a character with abstract powers, and I thought it would be a great place to put this theme."

ALL IMAGES: **QIU FANG**

SUBJECT
SIGMA

Like all skins, the designers sought a unique twist to put on the character. "Every skin has to be different at the end of the day. Just making the colors or the shapes a little different is not enough," said Fang. "We're always trying to find some kind of unique twist—a new interaction of shapes or construction that still fills in the basic volume of the hero but gives you a completely different take on it."

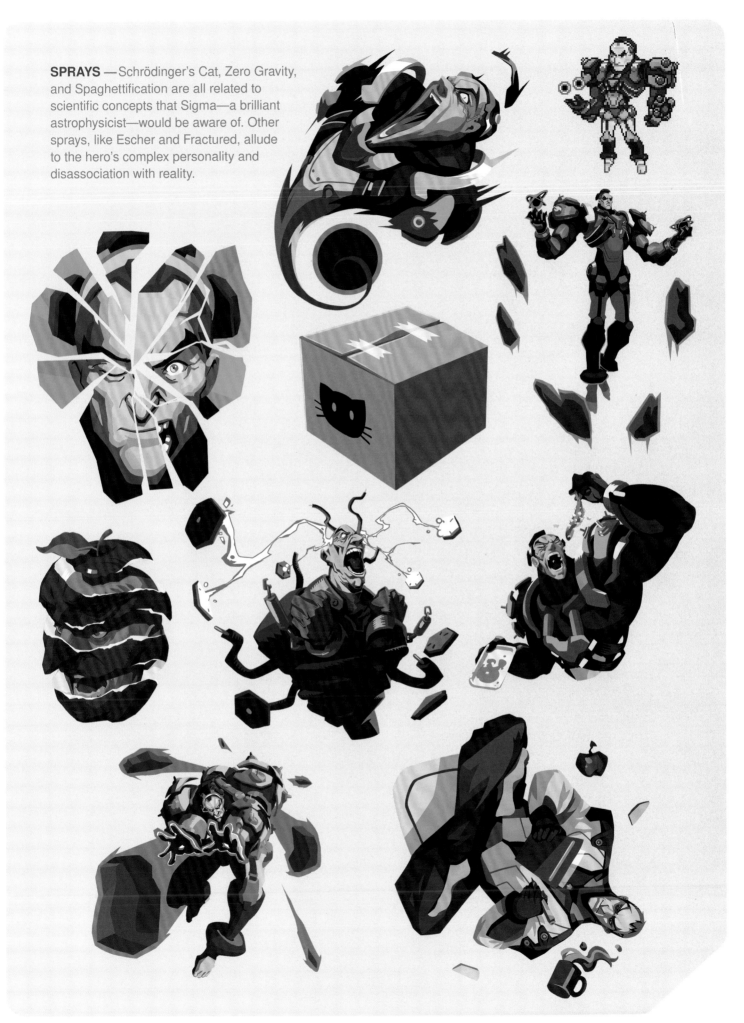

SPRAYS —Schrödinger's Cat, Zero Gravity, and Spaghettification are all related to scientific concepts that Sigma—a brilliant astrophysicist—would be aware of. Other sprays, like Escher and Fractured, allude to the hero's complex personality and disassociation with reality.

BEN ZHANG, ARNOLD TSANG, QIU FANG, AQUATIC MOON, ANH DANG, MORTEN SKAALVIK, AND DARYL TAN

ORIGIN STORY —In crafting Sigma's origin story, the team faced strict limitations. Time was short, and the filmmakers wouldn't be able to use the same number of illustrations that they had for previous pieces. On top of that, they were dealing with a character whose backstory and mindset were very abstract. The team wanted to make sure that Sigma didn't come across as insane—the truth was that he had become disconnected from reality and time.

"We thought, 'Okay, that's a lot to convey in a very short amount of time and with limited resources,'" said the piece's director, Jeramiah Johnson. "So we were just jamming on ideas one day, and I had this bizarre idea—what if we tell it in a different way than we usually do?"

Thinking outside the box led Johnson and the team to create one of the most memorable origin stories to date. With only a small number of images at their disposal, the filmmakers combined different parts of each illustration, swapping backgrounds and characters to create a sense of reality breaking down around Sigma. It was the perfect way to convey his emotional and mental state. Through this resourceful combination of images, the team also created a clear story arc for the character, showing the path his life took before he became a part of Talon.

One of the keys to success was an early edit created by Johnson, editor Michael Bancroft, writer Andrew Robinson, and artist Nesskain. They used this rough cut of the story to prove to the rest of the team that the idea could work. For Nesskain, seeing this early edit told him everything he needed to know about what would be required for the illustrations.

"I gave them the storyboards. It was just character with no backgrounds at the time," said Nesskain. "Once they did the edit, it was easy for me to see what was possible after that."

ECHO

Sleek and futuristic, Echo's design evokes the qualities of *Overwatch*'s bright and aspirational future. As a character, she also plays into the game's themes: she is a force for good, a member of the Overwatch organization who is dedicated to protecting those in need with her unique abilities.

Echo was released on March 18, 2020, but her origins stretch back long before the game came out. Her general look was based on robots created for the unreleased Project Titan, the predecessor to *Overwatch*. "When we picked heroes for the initial *Overwatch* lineup, we threw in one of those bots because it showed a futuristic side of the franchise," said character art director Arnold Tsang. "We called her 'Athena Bot' for the longest time."

This early version of Echo first appeared in an illustration from the announcement cinematic, but the team wasn't ready to flesh out her backstory or turn her into a hero. It wasn't until they created the Route 66 map that they seriously considered developing the character more.

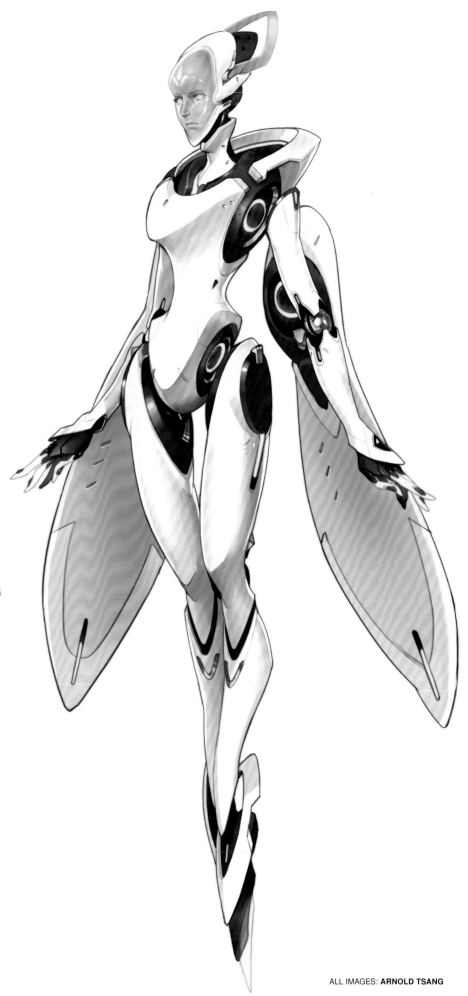

ALL IMAGES: **ARNOLD TSANG**

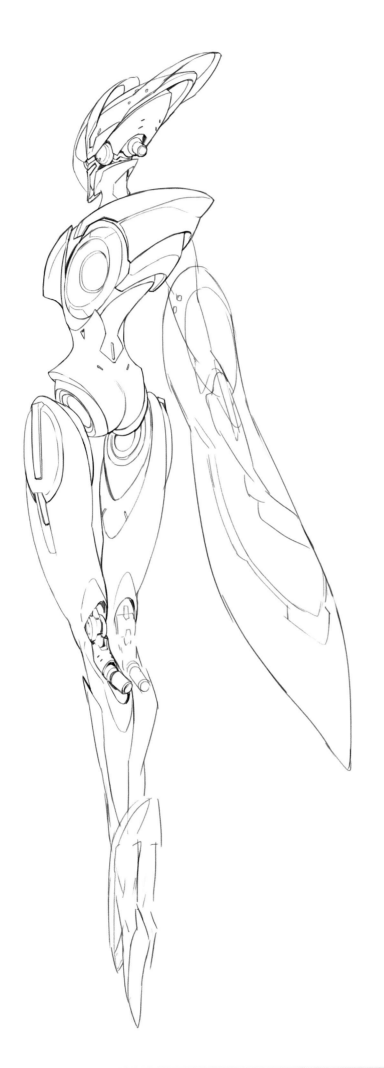

"The first time we thought about having her in the fiction was with the 'egg'—the super high-tech payload on the Route 66 map," said Tsang. "Because of the design choices we made for the egg, it made sense Echo would be in there."

Tsang created a set of early sketches to explore where the team could go with Echo if they decided to turn her into a hero. First and foremost, the designers wanted to give the character a face, which would help players connect with her. Tsang tried different variations, including one that turned the energy shield from the original design into something more humanlike.

As her look was being fleshed out, the team also developed her backstory. Due to her connection with the payload on Route 66, McCree's old stomping grounds, the team imagined that she had a relationship with the gunslinger. This was explored in the "Reunion" animated short, which depicted McCree releasing Echo from the payload and urging her to seek out Winston.

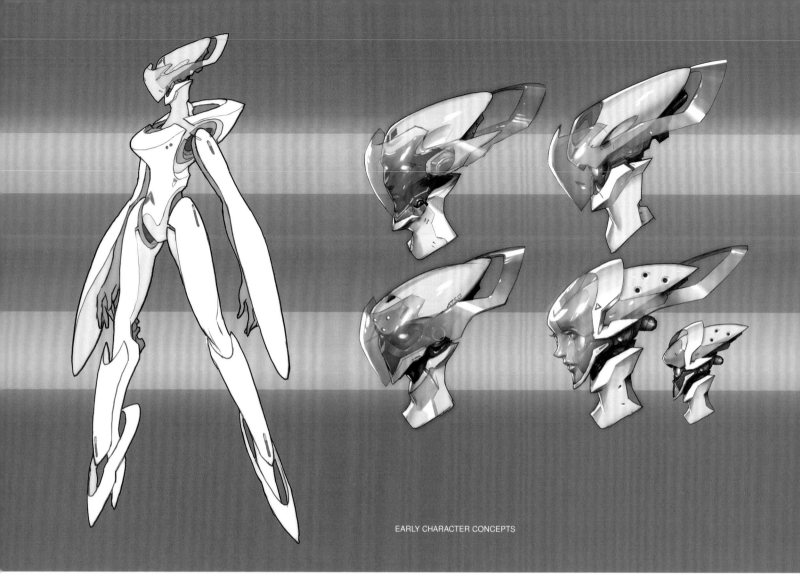

EARLY CHARACTER CONCEPTS

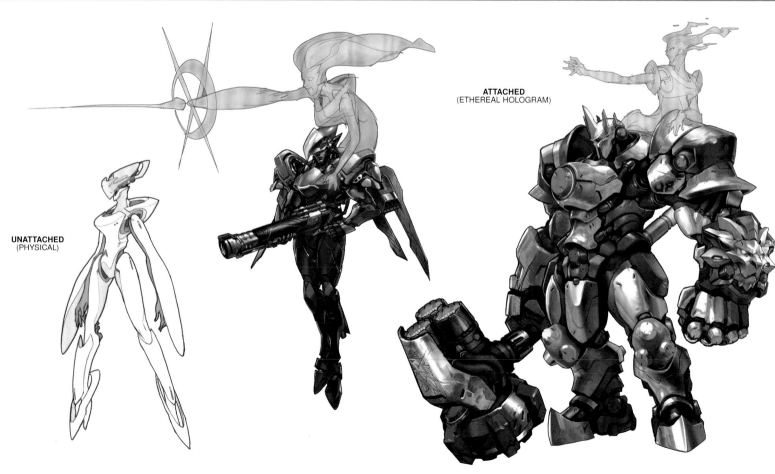

UNATTACHED
(PHYSICAL)

ATTACHED
(ETHEREAL HOLOGRAM)

ALL IMAGES: **ARNOLD TSANG**

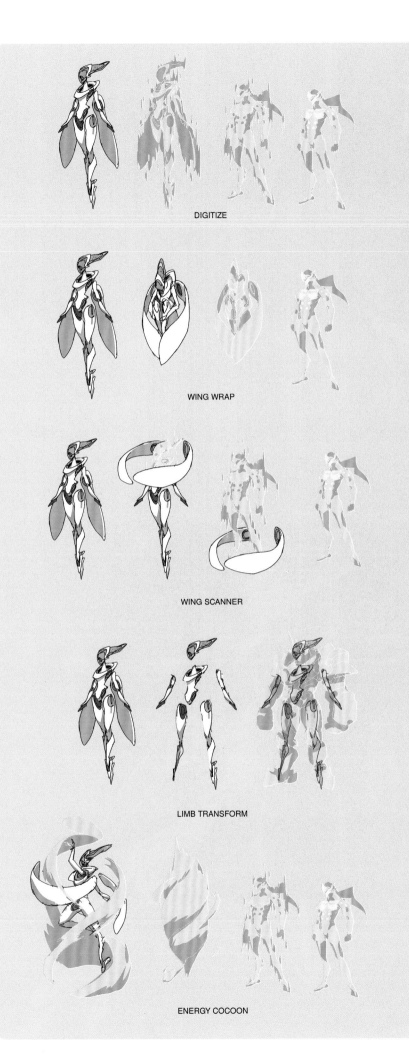

DIGITIZE

WING WRAP

WING SCANNER

LIMB TRANSFORM

ENERGY COCOON

▶ **ECHO'S ROLE –** One of the main issues the team faced was deciding what role Echo would play in the game itself. Was she a support? A damage dealer? The designers didn't start answering these questions until the final stages of the hero's development.

An early version of Echo's gameplay style depicted her as a support character who physically attached to other heroes. She would act as something of a turret, moving with the other character. The team ultimately moved away from this idea in favor of something far different but no less unique.

"Her name comes from the desire to make her a mimic bot—a shapeshifter-type character. The original idea was that Echo was a reincarnation of the scientist who created her. But she's a simulation—not completely that person," said character art director Arnold Tsang.

Based on this idea of a mimic bot, the designers decided that Echo would work best as a damage dealer instead of a support. She would be able to shapeshift and copy the abilities of other heroes. This presented technical challenges, like those that arose when the team created B.O.B. as Ashe's ultimate ability. The game is designed to support six different characters in a match on each team, but when Echo morphed into someone else, it would technically mean another hero was joining the game.

While the team found solutions to deal with these technical constraints, concept artist Qiu Fang sketched designs to explore the look of Echo's transformation and how it would integrate into gameplay. He tried different versions, including some where Echo's limbs detach and form into the skeleton of the hero she mimics.

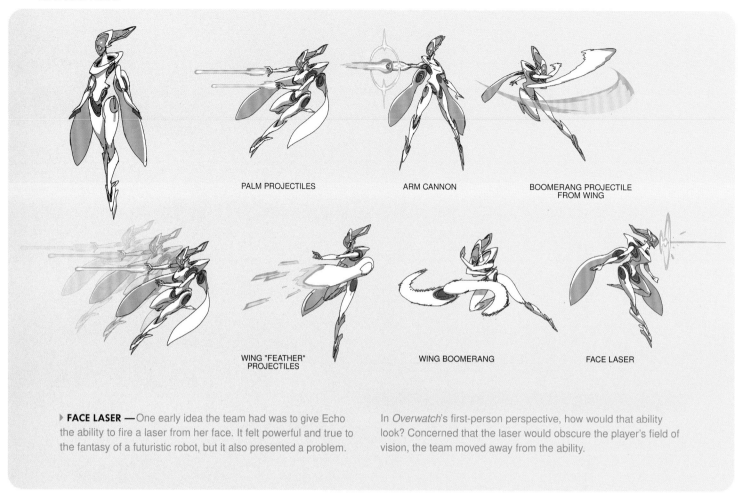

PALM PROJECTILES

ARM CANNON

BOOMERANG PROJECTILE
FROM WING

WING "FEATHER"
PROJECTILES

WING BOOMERANG

FACE LASER

▶ **FACE LASER** —One early idea the team had was to give Echo the ability to fire a laser from her face. It felt powerful and true to the fantasy of a futuristic robot, but it also presented a problem.

In *Overwatch*'s first-person perspective, how would that ability look? Concerned that the laser would obscure the player's field of vision, the team moved away from the ability.

Echo's appearance in the short predated her release as a playable hero. Though she was only on screen for a relatively short time, the developers paid close attention to her appearance and animation style. "We spent a lot of time developing her movement. When she's acting, she's effortless, and she has slower gestures," said the game's lead animator, Ryan Denniston. "So you can still feel the machine part of her, but it's like the high-end version of a machine. You think of Bastion as an older type, and Echo is the most cutting-edge machine that you could ever imagine."

Even after "Reunion" was released, work on Echo's design did not cease. As the developers finalized her in-game abilities, they discovered that some aspects of her appearance would need to change. "We didn't want her to carry a weapon, necessarily. She can shapeshift, so her body is the weapon," said former lead character artist Renaud Galand. "That brought its fair share of challenges. Looking at the original design, we needed to do something to convey a little bit more of that aspect of her. Especially when she settled down and decided she would fire with her fingers, we had to reengineer and redesign that side so it wouldn't just look like a simple glove."

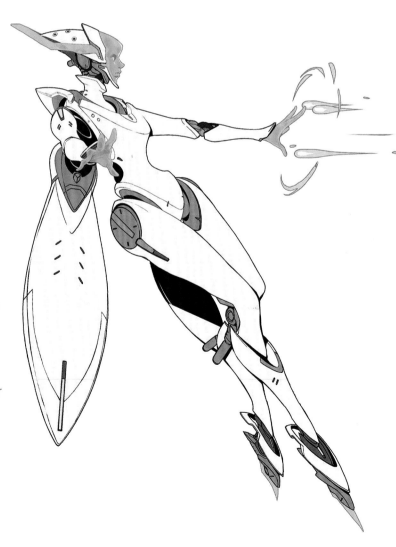

TOP: **ARNOLD TSANG**; BOTTOM: **MANUEL DISCHINGER**

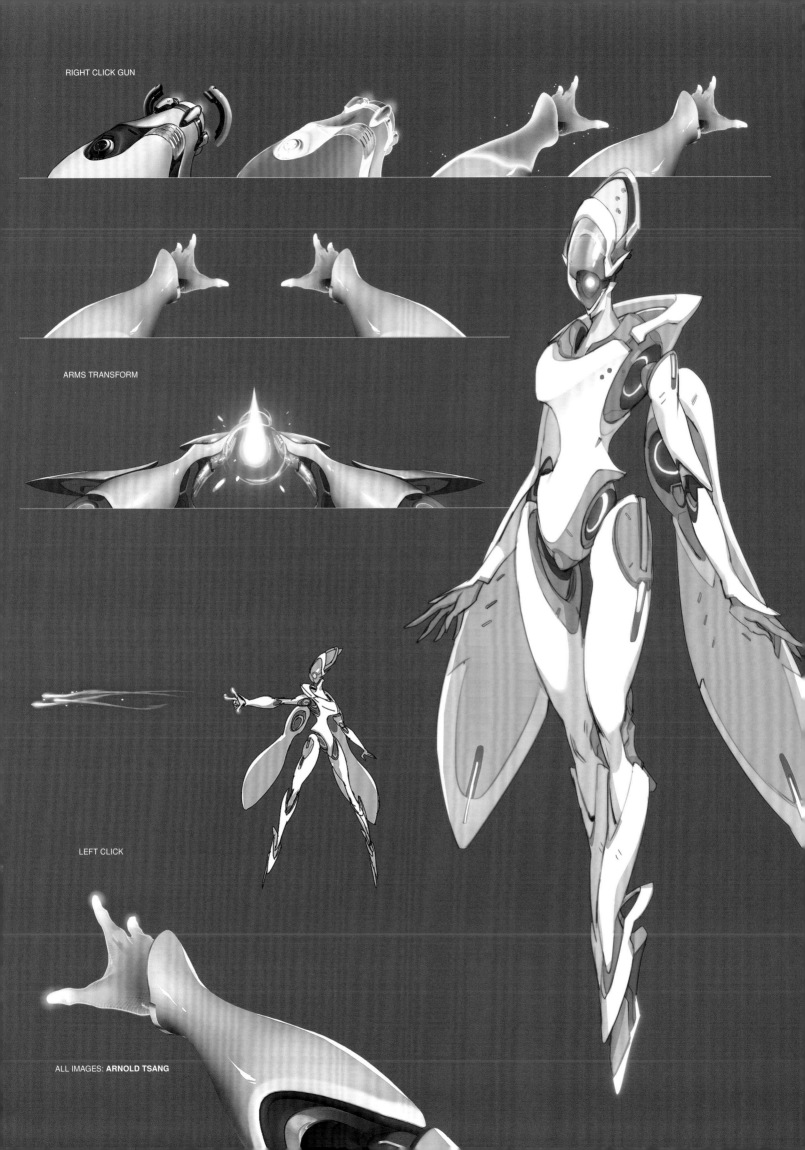

RIGHT CLICK GUN

ARMS TRANSFORM

LEFT CLICK

ALL IMAGES: **ARNOLD TSANG**

STEALTH

MOTH

SKINS —One of Echo's notable abilities is that she can fly, and this heavily influenced her Moth skin. "What kind of skin ideas let us play with Echo's wings a little bit?" said Fang, who designed the skin. "A moth has similar-shaped wings."

Echo's Stealth skin approached the hero with a polar opposite goal from Moth. While the latter featured fur and other organic textures, the former embraced the character's mechanical side. Stealth is a reimagining of Echo as a machine with sharper edges—even her face is replaced by a targeting reticle.

LEFT: **ARNOLD TSANG**; RIGHT: **QIU FANG**

SPRAYS — Many of Echo's sprays pay homage to iconic science-fiction movies and anime. They also draw on elements from her past, such as her relationship with the scientist who created her. Daryl Tan, who worked on some of the sprays, approached these sprays differently from other pieces of art, such as character concepts.

"There are no soft edges in the sprays—they're all just hard shapes," said Tan. "You can have as many shapes as you want—as long as they read graphically, then you're good. Because the spray is going to be on a wall, it has to read well from far away—that's the biggest rule we have for the sprays."

DARYL TAN, ANH DANG, ARNOLD TSANG, QIU FANG, TIM GUO, AND **JONATHAN RYDER**

ORIGIN STORY —Echo's origin story explores the hero as well as her creator, Dr. Mina Liao. It was important for the team to depict the doctor's death in the cinematic, thereby explaining why she is no longer around. But it was just as important to show *who* Liao was so that it would provide context for Echo's identity.

Over the course of the story, the filmmakers highlighted important moments from Liao's past. They showed her as one of the creators of omnics and an early member of the Overwatch organization. Using only a few images, they carved out a big place for her in the lore, which also gave Echo a sense of history and purpose.

ALL IMAGES: **NESSKAIN**

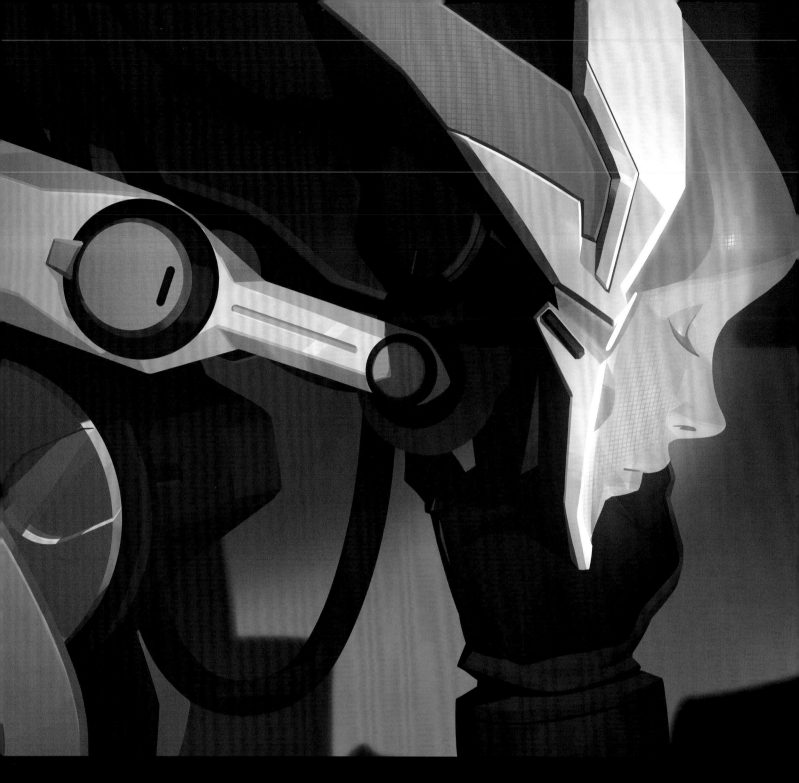

"You're reliving it all in this piece, so we thought this was a way to show her history and say goodbye to Mina," said the cinematic's director, Doug Gregory. "But it also works as Echo's origin story."

Gregory and the team pushed the motion-story medium into new territory to convey these moments from Liao's life. The origin piece features a "bullet time" effect where the camera slowly moves around shards of glass that reflect important scenes from the character's past. This technique makes the origin story feel more like a 3-D film.

"We had to circle around the character, so it had to feel like it was an animation, but with very few

frames," said artist Nesskain, who created images for the piece. "There were only a few illustrations. The motion-story team helped me a lot with that— they gave me a 3-D map of the space with the character, and I just picked three moments where they stretch out the illustration to feel like it's a full animation."

For Nesskain, the use of color remained a crucial part of telling the story. In the final two illustrations of Echo, he balanced light and shadow to accentuate the blue on her face and also give the sense that she is sleeping. As the hero comes online at the end, Nesskain brought in more light to indicate Echo is waking up.

OVERLORD TRANSPORT

MURKY L...

BLACKROCK MOUNTAIN

JOURNEY TO AIUR

DARKMOON FAIRE

ZEPPELIN LANDING

DARKMOON FERRIS WHEEL

GATES OF ORGRIMMAR

MURLOC ISLAND

SNAXXRAMAS

BOOT BAY

THE FARGODEEP MINE

BLACKHEART'S REVENGE

THE HELLSCREAM

SIEGE OF ORGRIMMAR

STONE CAIRN LAKE

LOST AND FOUND VIKINGS

THE MAGE DISTRICT

MOONWELL

WIZARD'S SANCTUM MAGIC SHOW

HEARTHSTONE TA...

P

LURKY PARKING LOT

KHADGAR'S HERBS

BLIZZARDWORLD

BLIZZAR...

DEEPRUN TRAM

TYRAEL'S FALL

DEN OF EVIL

O CENTER
OFF

TRISTRAM
ATHEDRAL

GHOST
ACADEMY

FLIGHT TO
DUSKWOOD

PYLO
TERRA

ANCIENT
CURIOS

ESCAPE FR
STOCK

AUC

LD

ENVIRONMENTS

One of *Overwatch*'s core themes is the idea of a future worth fighting for. Many of the heroes symbolize this value, and so do the game's environments. Part of *Overwatch*'s allure is that it takes players to cities and locations around the world, where they can experience the beauty of Earth's diverse cultures and a hopeful vision for their future.

In 2017, there were many cities and countries the designers still wanted to see in the game's stylized aesthetic. Based on the success of previous maps, they had learned lessons on how to make this content even more impactful for the community. "The maps that resonated more were the ones that connected to a character or the lore of *Overwatch*. For example, King's Row and Tracer," said associate art director Dion Rogers. "With the new maps, we made an effort to find ones that connected to characters."

The team had learned other lessons as well. From analyzing previous environments, they realized that the game looks best in bright, directional light. They identified and focused on the iconic elements of each location, and they removed extraneous detail that might overwhelm players or clutter the environment, especially during action-packed battles.

BLIZZARD WORLD

What if a Blizzard-themed amusement park existed in *Overwatch*? What would it look like? What kind of rides would it have? These questions were buzzing around the team as they brainstormed ideas for the Blizzard World map, which was released at BlizzCon on November 3, 2017.

"Blizzard World was really special to a lot of people on the team," said art director Bill Petras. "It was a fun and exciting way to bring all these franchises that we love into *Overwatch*."

BOTTOM: **BEN ZHANG**; TOP: **AQUATIC MOON**

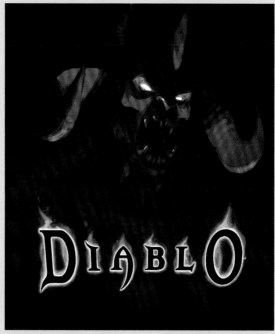

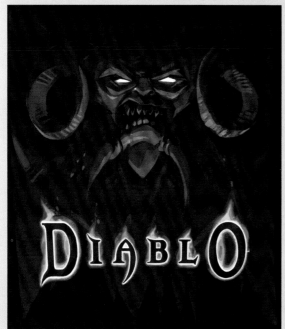

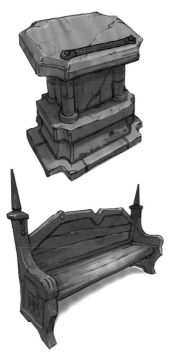

THRONE
CONCEPT

DIABLO ALTAR

TOP: **OSCAR CAFARO**; BOTTOM: **AQUATIC MOON**

RIDE POSTERS

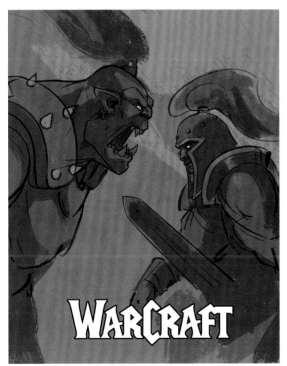

TOP LEFT: **AQUATIC MOON**; MIDDLE LEFT: **GLEN BROGAN** FOR **HERO COMPLEX GALLERY**; MIDDLE: **OSCAR CAFARO**; TOP RIGHT: **LLIA YU**; BOTTOM: **OSCAR CAFARO**

RIDE WITH THE SKELETON KING

BLIZZARDWORLD

OVERLORD TRANSPORT

MURKY PARKING LOT

TYRAEL'S FALL

SHEN'S DELIGHTS

BLACKROCK MOUNTAIN

COMMAND CENTER LIFT OFF

DEN OF EVIL

CALDEUM MARKET

DARKMOON FAIRE

JOURNEY TO AIUR

TRISTRAM CATHEDRAL

THE SLAUGHTERED CALF INN

ZEPPELIN LANDING

GATES OF ORGRIMMAR

NEW TRISTRAM

DARKMOON FERRIS WHEEL

MURLOC ISLAND

SNAXXRAMAS

GHOST ACADEMY

REIGN OF THE BLACK KING

BOOTY BAY

FLIGHT TO DUSKWOOD

THE FARGODEEP MINE

HEROES ARCADE

THE HELLSCREAM

BLACKHEART'S REVENGE

THE HATCHERY PETTING ZOO

SIEGE OF ORGRIMMAR

STONE CAIRN LAKE

PYLON TERRACE

THE NEXUS EXPERIENCE

NYDUS WORM SLIDE

THE MAGE DISTRICT

LOST AND FOUND VIKINGS

ANCIENT CURIOS

MOONWELL

PESTLE'S APOTHECARY

LURKY PARKING LOT

WIZARD'S SANCTUM MAGIC SHOW

HEARTHSTONE TAVERN

ESCAPE FROM THE STOCKADE

SPAWNING POOLS WATER PARK

KHADGAR'S HERBS

BLIZZARD WORLD

AUCTION HOUSE GIFT SHOP

DEEPRUN TRAM

GURKY PARKING LOT

With so much rich history surrounding Warcraft, StarCraft, Diablo, Hearthstone, and Blizzard's other universes, the designers had a wealth of material to draw from. The challenge they faced was choosing what they should focus on. Real amusement parks are enormous, and *Overwatch*'s maps are much smaller in comparison. To help with this task, the designers reached out to the teams responsible for making Blizzard's other games and asked them what they would want to see in Blizzard World. From the answers they received, they homed in on a handful of favorites: a few iconic places from *World of Warcraft* (including Naxxramus, Orgrimmar, Stormwind, and the Darkmoon Faire), a mix of terran, zerg, and protoss units from *StarCraft*, a Skeleton King–themed dungeon from *Diablo*, and a *Hearthstone* tavern.

RIDE POSTERS

TOP LEFT: **AQUATIC MOON;** TOP RIGHT, BOTTOM LEFT AND MIDDLE: **GLEN BROGAN** FOR **HERO COMPLEX GALLERY**; RIGHT: **LLIA YU**

MORE DESKS IF NEEDED

CONTROL ROOM INTERIOR IDEATION

TERMINAL CONCEPTS

Unfortunately, they had to pass on many of the other great ideas they received, either because there wasn't enough room to fit them in the environment or they would have proved too difficult to pull off. For example, the designers toyed with creating the Gates of Orgrimmar, but they were concerned that if players saw a gate, they would assume they could go through it, which they wouldn't actually be able to do. The team didn't abandon these concepts completely, though—some of them, like the Gates of Orgrimmar, are featured on an in-world map shown in the amusement park.

Apart from bringing elements of Blizzard's other worlds into the map, the designers also wanted to play with the fantasy of an amusement park. "We created two layers to the environment— what visitors see and what theme park workers see," said Rogers. "The payload itself is part of this theme. The story behind it is that the Skeleton King's helmet is being delivered to the *Diablo*-themed section of the amusement park."

TOP: **OSCAR CAFARO**; BOTTOM: **AL CRUTCHLEY**

ALL IMAGES: **AQUATIC MOON**

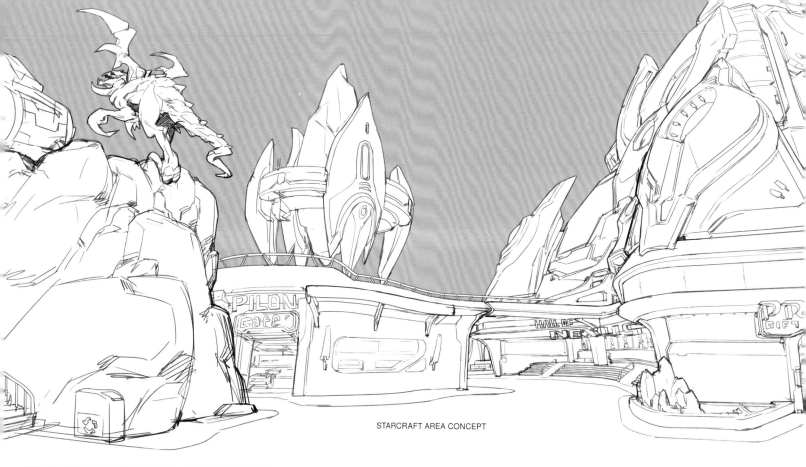

STARCRAFT AREA CONCEPT

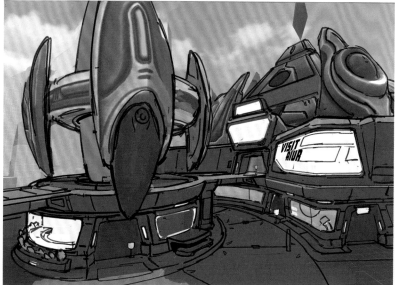

NEXUS CONCEPTS

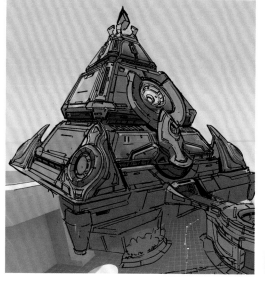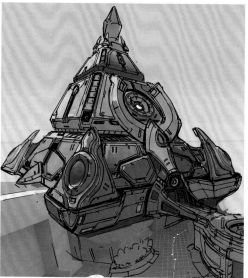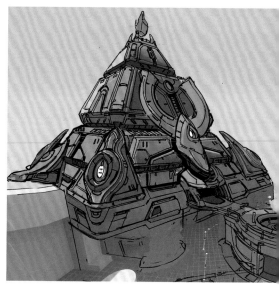

TOP LEFT: **BEN ZHANG**; MIDDLE AND BOTTOM LEFT: **AL CRUTCHLEY**; RIGHT: **AQUATIC MOON**

The fantasy of Blizzard World extended beyond the game map. To accompany the map's release at BlizzCon, amusement park–themed paraphernalia was also created. Some of these items were T-shirts bearing slogans like "I Survived the Heallscream"—a reference to one of the Warcraft-themed rides at Blizzard World. The team also made physical prints of the in-world amusement park map.

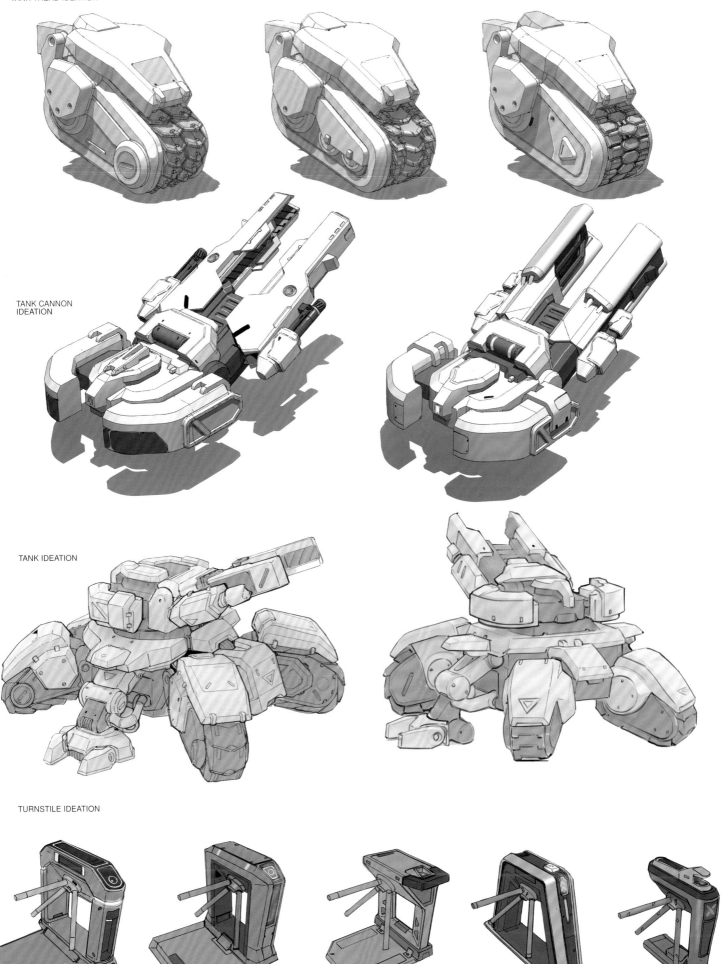

TANK TREAD IDEATION

TANK CANNON
IDEATION

TANK IDEATION

TURNSTILE IDEATION

TOP: **OSCAR CAFARO**; MIDDLE AND BOTTOM: **AL CRUTCHLEY**

AYUTTHAYA

There are many settings the designers want to bring into *Overwatch*, but they can't pursue every idea. This is partly due to time constraints—there are only so many new maps the team can make in a year. Thus, careful consideration is given to *why* they are creating the map. Ideally, the designers want to introduce environments that reveal deep, meaningful connections between the heroes and their world.

Thailand suffered from the latter issue. The team was eager to create a map based in that country, but there were no heroes or story connections to it. Eventually, the designers found an opportunity to explore Thailand as Capture the Flag map Ayutthaya, released on February 8, 2018.

"Capture the Flag maps are a chance to try places that don't need to be directly connected to the story of *Overwatch* or elements of the lore," said Rogers. "So for this one we chose Thailand."

The team channeled their passion into early concepts, envisioning Ayutthaya as a mirrored map, which has the same layout on each side. To make the experience unique for opposing teams, the designers created different aesthetics, manipulating color and architecture to make players feel as if they were in distinct locations.

"We wanted to make it unique so you can tell what side you're on," said Rogers. "One side was kind of a grand palace and the other was ancient ruins. But they each basically share the same positional data."

The designers gave each side of the map a characteristic look for gameplay reasons too. If players were running from the ruins to the grand palace or vice versa, they would get a sense of progression based on how the environment was changing around them.

ANCIENT TEMPLE EXTERIOR AND INTERIOR IDEATION

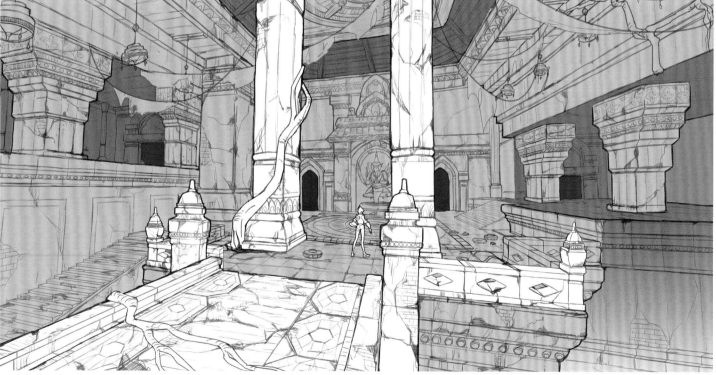

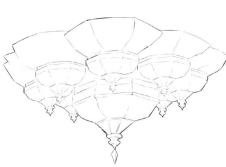

GOLD TEMPLE INTERIOR

FOUNTAIN CONCEPTS

JUNKERTOWN

Released on August 21, 2017, Junkertown occupies a special place among *Overwatch*'s vibrant and richly imagined environments. Unlike most other maps, it isn't based off a real-world location; it is uniquely rooted in the Overwatch universe. Junkertown is a fictional city built from the remnants of a destroyed omnium. Stylistically, the map also challenges *Overwatch*'s hopeful tone, drawing inspiration from postapocalyptic films and the game's more rough-and-tumble characters like Junkrat and Roadhog.

KANGAROO SUSHI

RIPPER

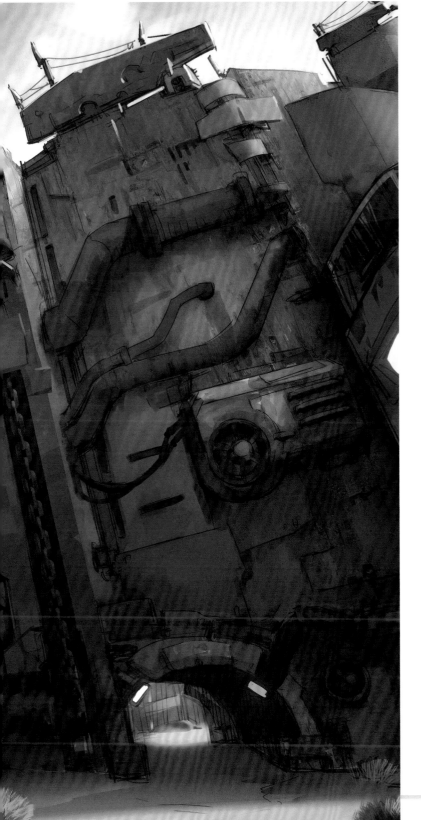

MARKET/
SHIPWRECK

MECHANICS
WORKSHOP

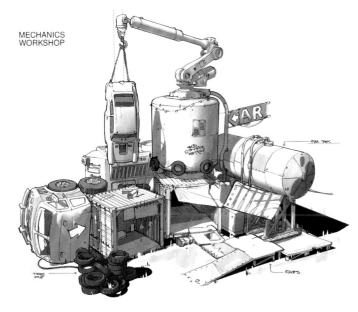

BOTTOM RIGHT: **BEN ZHANG**; RIGHT AND FAR LEFT: **OSCAR CAFARO**

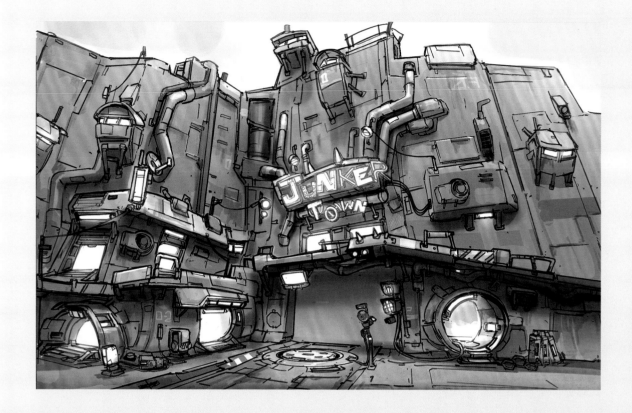

▶ **BEN'S CONCEPTS**—The designers initially struggled creating the gate at the entrance to Junkertown. They had a wealth of ideas, but they couldn't narrow in on a simple unified look. Former concept artist Ben Zhang gathered many of these early ideas and combined them into a single rough sketch. The colors, materials, and lighting scheme in this image helped guide the team as they created the rest of Junkertown.

"Most of the environment concepts I did, I always approached from real game- and level-design feedback. Before I start touching these things, we already have the environment artists blocking these spaces out," said Zhang. "I roughly know how high the gate is and where the entrance is. These things give me a lot of good ideas for how to approach the concept."

SCRAPYARD CONCEPTS

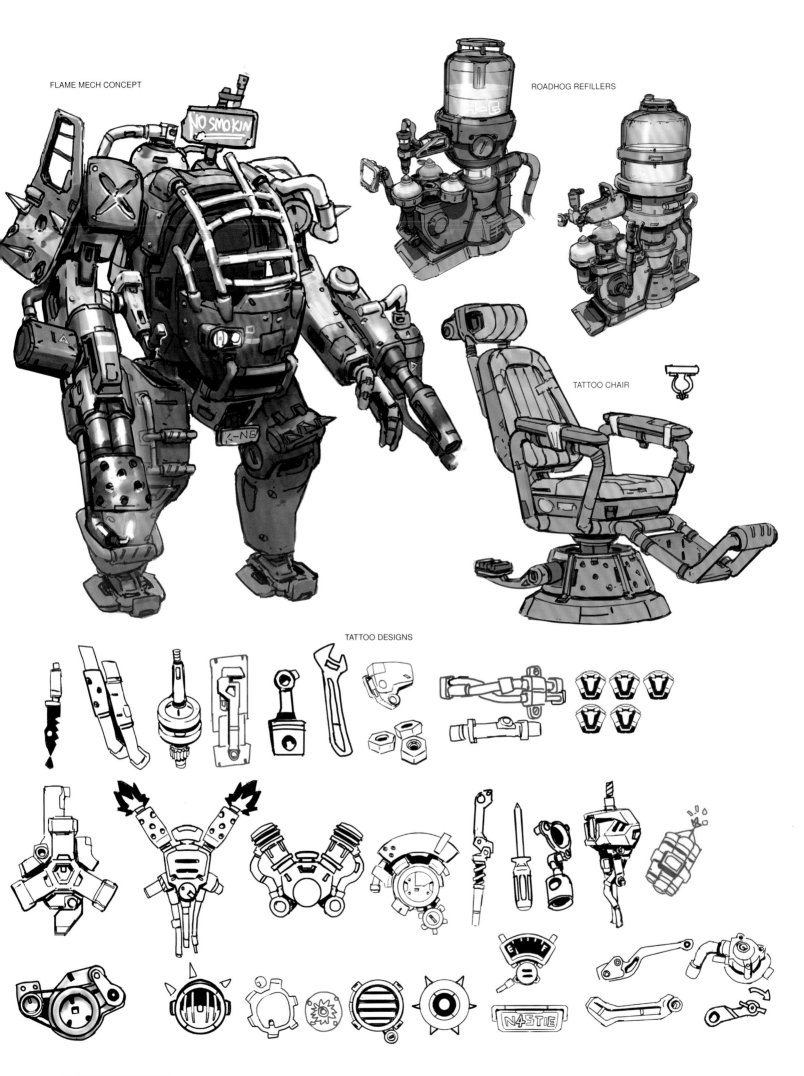

FLAME MECH CONCEPT

NO SMOKIN

ROADHOG REFILLERS

TATTOO CHAIR

TATTOO DESIGNS

N4STIE

ALL IMAGES: **AL CRUTCHLEY**

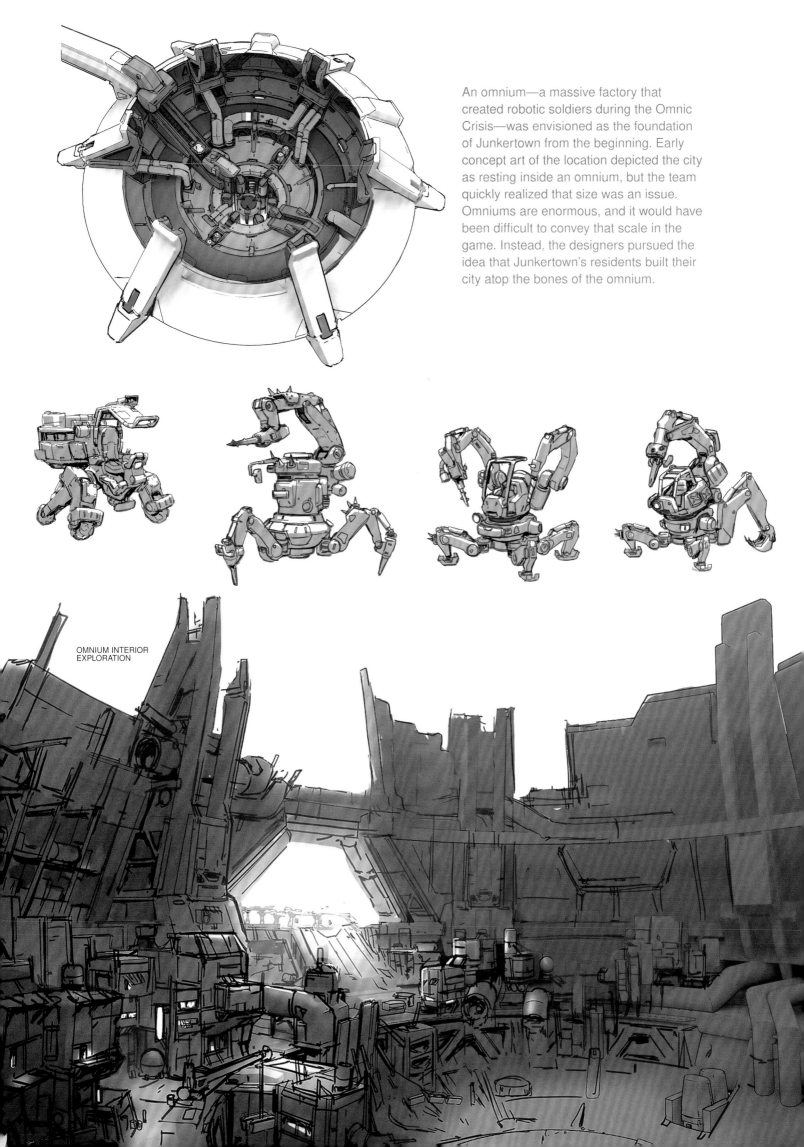

An omnium—a massive factory that created robotic soldiers during the Omnic Crisis—was envisioned as the foundation of Junkertown from the beginning. Early concept art of the location depicted the city as resting inside an omnium, but the team quickly realized that size was an issue. Omniums are enormous, and it would have been difficult to convey that scale in the game. Instead, the designers pursued the idea that Junkertown's residents built their city atop the bones of the omnium.

OMNIUM INTERIOR
EXPLORATION

Colors and shapes draw a distinction between what came from the omnium and what was scrap that the people of Junkertown brought in from the outside. Props featuring more angular and uniform geometry give the impression of advanced technology, which contrasts with the rusty metal that covers most of the environment.

This disparity between levels of technology extends to buildings outside the city as well. Junkertown was designed as a payload map, and one of the team's fundamental design goals was to create three visually distinct areas for each phase of gameplay. That way, players have a sense of progression as they push the payload through the map.

OMNIUM EXPLORATION

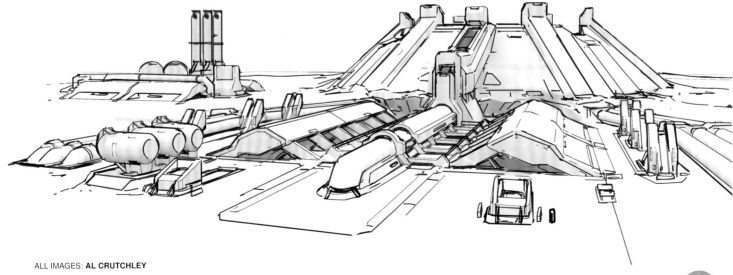

ALL IMAGES: **AL CRUTCHLEY**

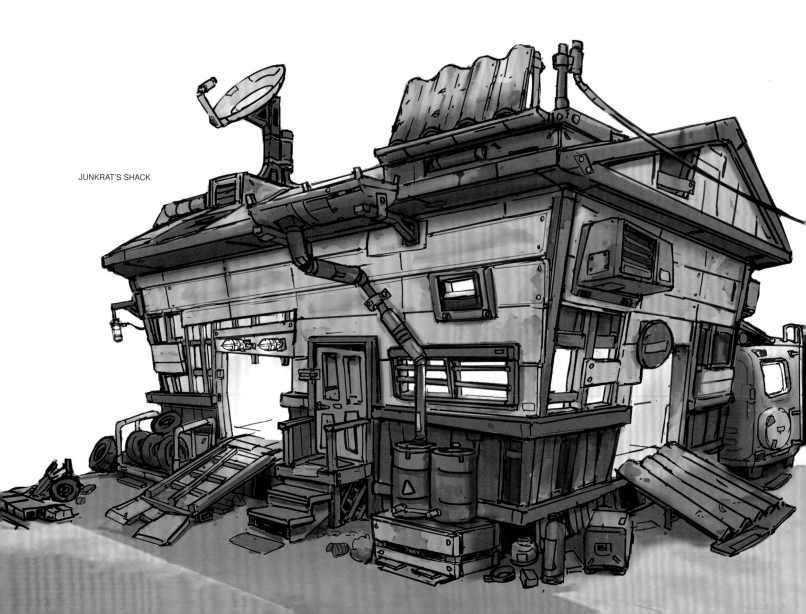

JUNKRAT'S SHACK

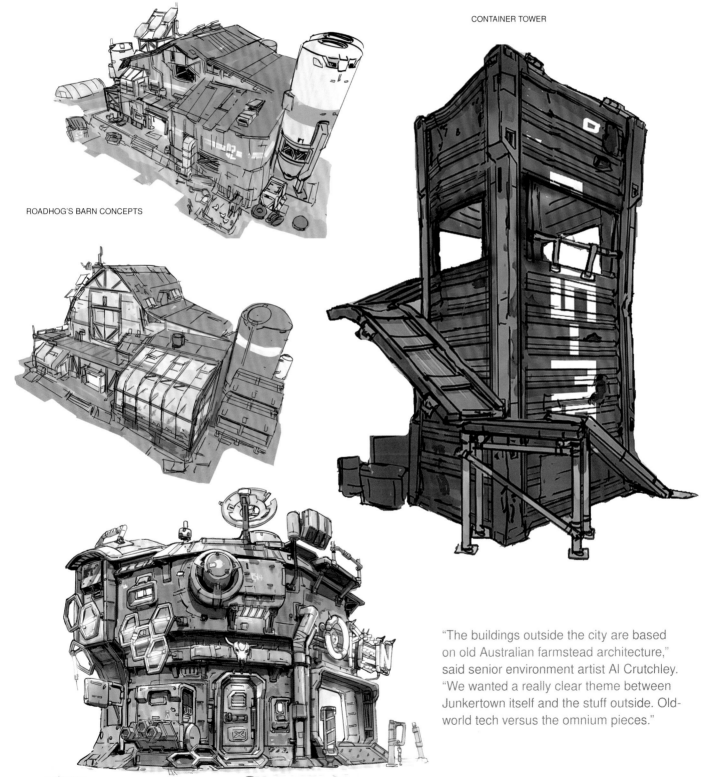

CONTAINER TOWER

ROADHOG'S BARN CONCEPTS

"The buildings outside the city are based on old Australian farmstead architecture," said senior environment artist Al Crutchley. "We wanted a really clear theme between Junkertown itself and the stuff outside. Old-world tech versus the omnium pieces."

ALL IMAGES: **AL CRUTCHLEY**

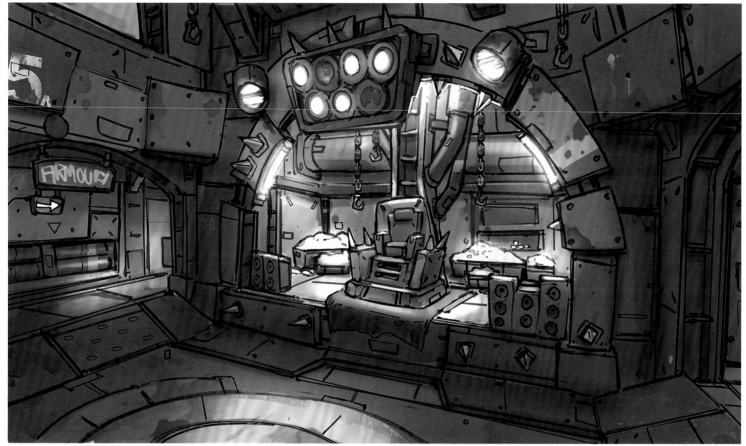

THRONE CONCEPTS

SIGNS

▶ **TAKE AWAY** —The original concept for the koala sign above by Oscar Cafaro said "take-out." When the Junkertown map was released, the community pointed out that in Australia, the phrase used is "take-away." The team then adjusted the in-game sign to make it more accurate.

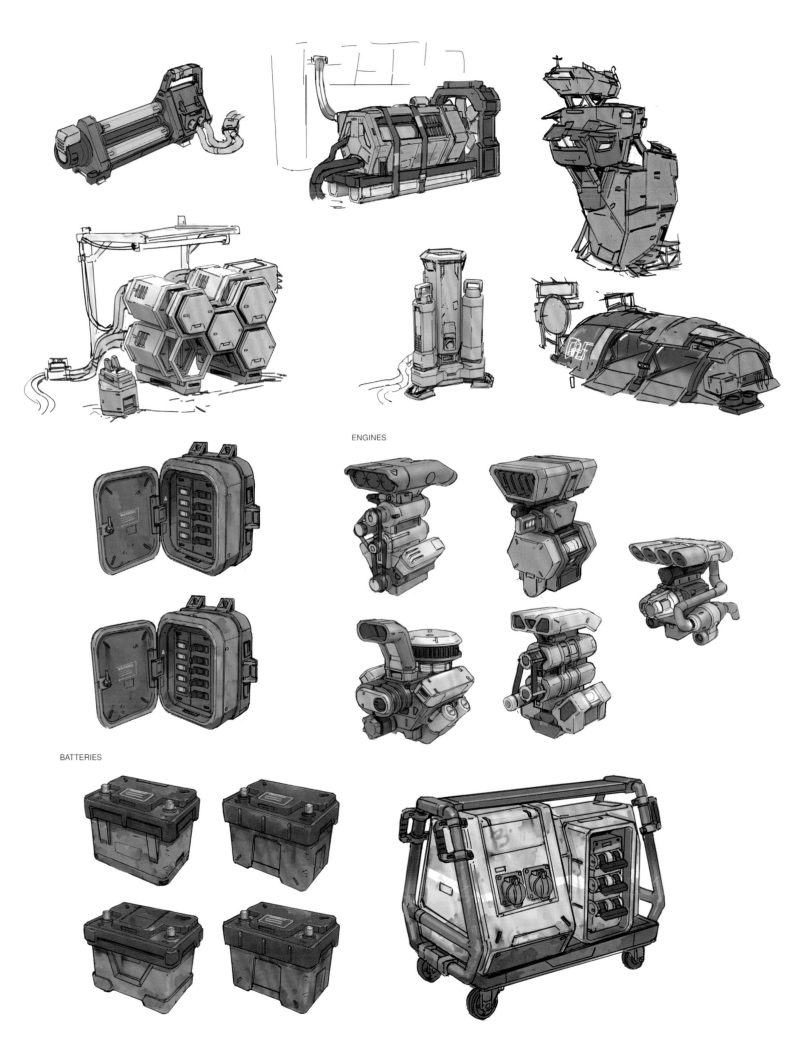

ENGINES

BATTERIES

ALL IMAGES: **AL CRUTCHLEY**; OPPOSITE, BOTTOM RIGHT: **OSCAR CAFARO**

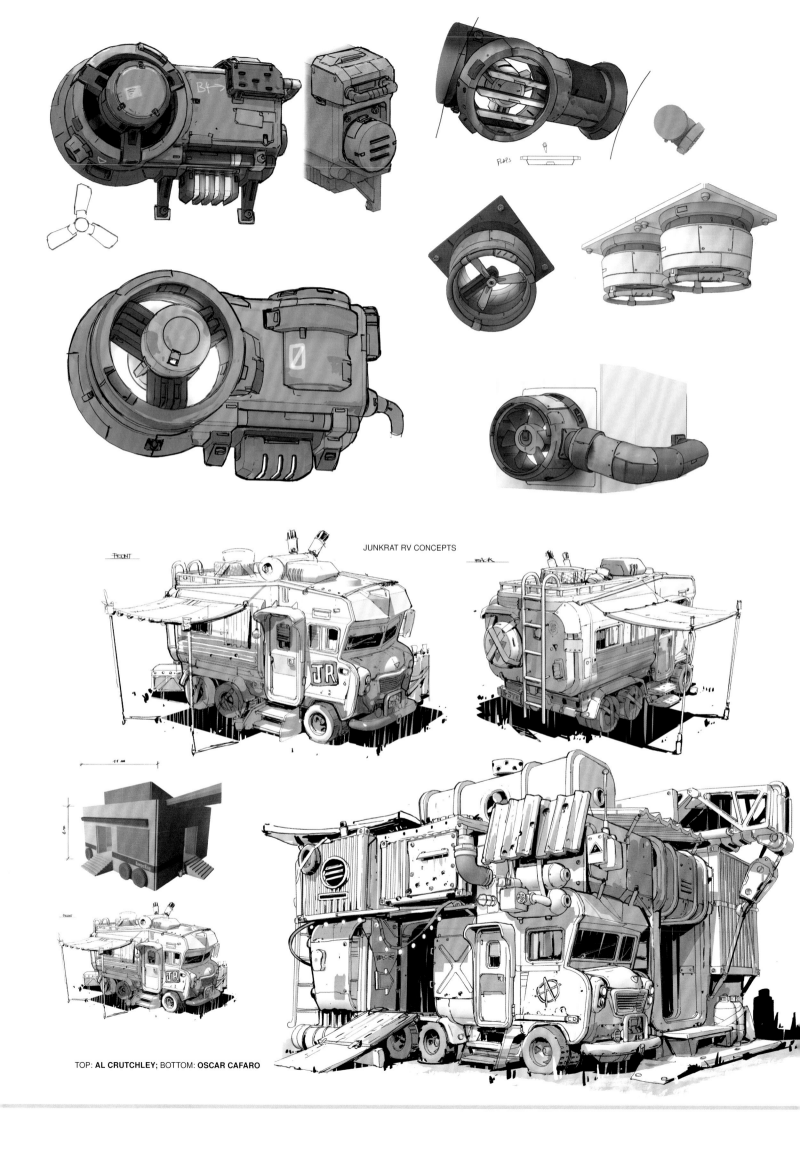

JUNKRAT RV CONCEPTS

TOP: **AL CRUTCHLEY**; BOTTOM: **OSCAR CAFARO**

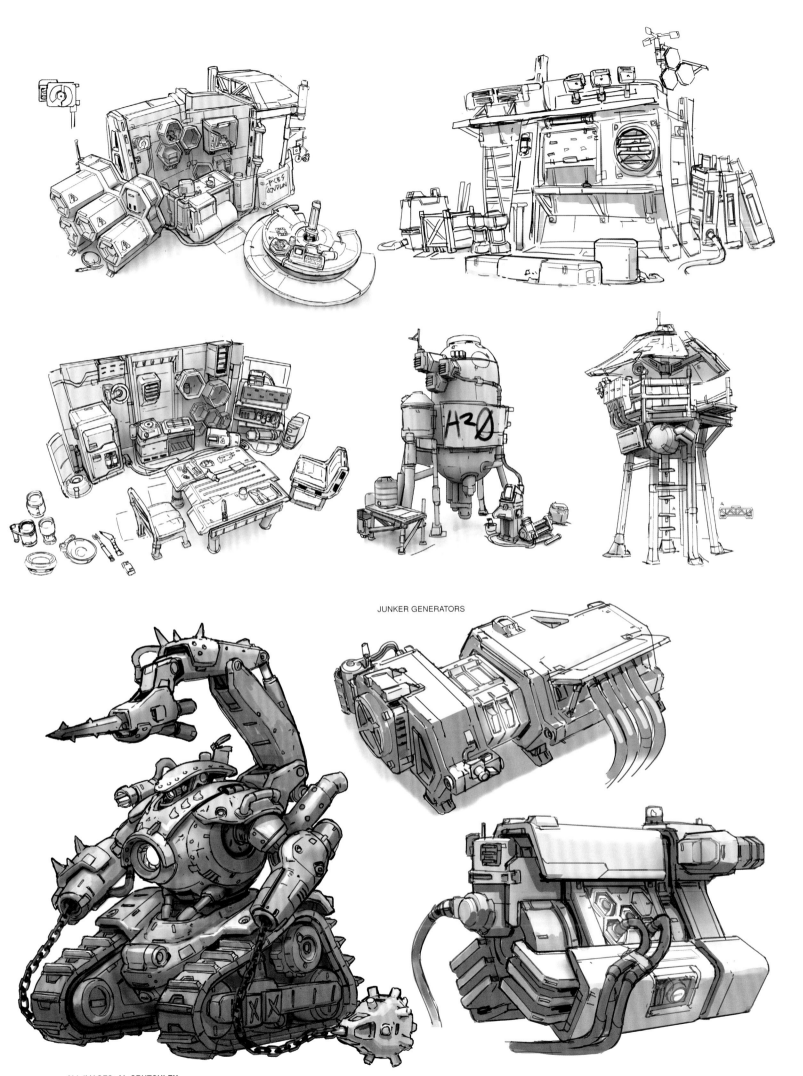

JUNKER GENERATORS

ALL IMAGES: **AL CRUTCHLEY**

"THE PLAN"

To accompany the release of Junkertown, the team created a cinematic featuring Junkrat and Roadhog. The main goal was to get people excited about the new environment, but this project was also an opportunity to create *Overwatch*'s first in-game cinematic (IGC). Unlike the prerendered animated shorts like "Rise and Shine" and "Honor and Glory,"

or the 2.5-D origin story shorts, the IGCs utilize the power of the game engine itself.

"They tend to be a little bit higher speed. We can make movies within a shorter timeframe because we get to utilize what exists in the game," said Terran Gregory, who directed "The Plan."

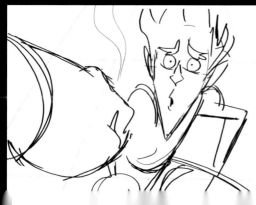

A primary goal for the IGCs was to create a seamless look between the films and the game itself. "We don't want to redefine the game," said Gregory. "We want to show it in its best possible light."

Based on this philosophy, the filmmakers used as many assets directly from the game as they could. Small adjustments were made to characters where necessary, such as using higher-resolution textures and reworking the geometry of their faces to allow for a wider range of expressions. These techniques would be used in the production of future *Overwatch* IGCs, such as for the Retribution and Storm Rising Archives missions. "The Plan" laid the groundwork for many more films yet to come.

STORYBOARDS AND FINAL RENDERS

RIALTO

Released on April 4, 2018, the Rialto map is a beautiful reimagining of the central area of Venice, Italy. Two versions of the environment were created for the game: one for PVP (player-versus-player) mode and another for the Retribution PVE (player-versus-environment) mission. The team made adjustments to each map based on the needs of gameplay, but also to convey the location's importance to Overwatch history.

The powerful crime syndicate Talon has a base in Rialto, and the designers wanted the environment to say something about the organization and its sensibilities. "We had a chance to define them more than we had before," said Rogers. "Some of their members are very wealthy—from old money. What we wanted to get across is that they have taken over buildings in beautiful, historic places like Venice."

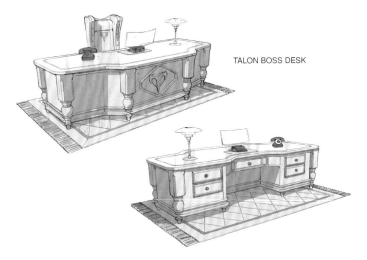

TALON BOSS DESK

Each version of Rialto offered different details about Talon's presence. In the PVE map, players are able to go deeper into the organization's secret base. In the PVP map, they are able to explore Talon's massive boardroom.

BOTTOM: **LLIA YU**; TOP: **OSCAR CAFARO**

In addition to finding the right places to layer in story elements, one of the biggest challenges the team faced was giving Rialto an *Overwatch* touch. "In developing the visual look of the maps, we ask ourselves what makes this environment unique to the Overwatch world?" said Petras. "We drained the canals at one point and had omnics working in them. In an earlier version, waterfalls were everywhere, and the canals were flooded. It was a fun exercise on how to develop the fantasy of Rialto for *Overwatch*, but ultimately we ended up somewhere in the middle."

HOTEL LOBBY

OPERA STORAGE

ALL IMAGES: **AL CRUTCHLEY**

TALON BASE

TOP: **AL CRUTCHLEY** ; BOTTOM: **OSCAR CAFARO**

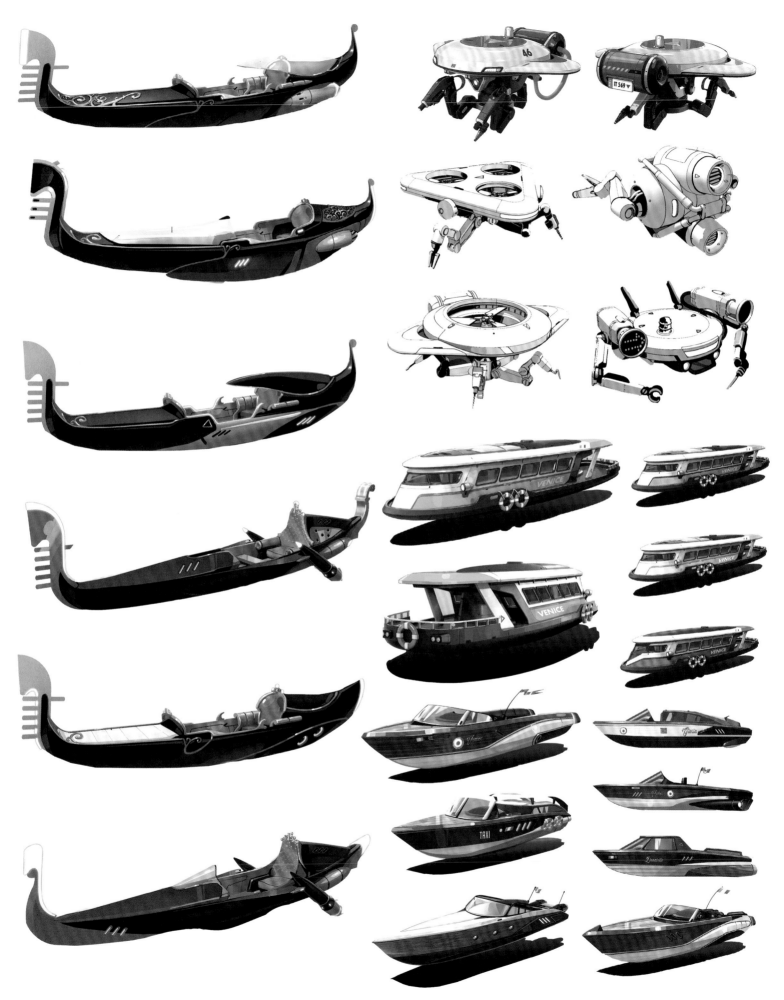

ALL IMAGES: **OSCAR CAFARO**

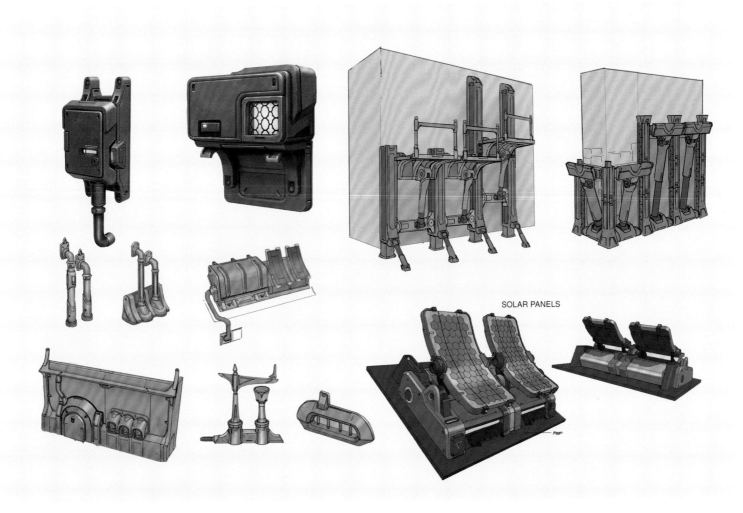

SOLAR PANELS

STREET PROPS

POSTE

NAME
NAME

NAME

NAME
NAME
NAME

ALL IMAGES: **AL CRUTCHLEY**

PETRA

Most of *Overwatch*'s environments are based on cityscapes, so the team is always excited by the rare "organic map"—a location primarily composed of natural formations like forests, water, or stone. Petra, with its beautiful sandstone cliffs and carvings, was a chance for the designers to discover what a rocky environment would look like in *Overwatch*'s stylized world.

Released on May 9, 2018, Petra had no existing ties to heroes or the game's story, but the team added connections through an archaeological group present in the map. "They are assumed to be the same people who are exploring the top level of Ilios," said associate art director Dion Rogers, referring to a previously released map set in the Aegean Sea.

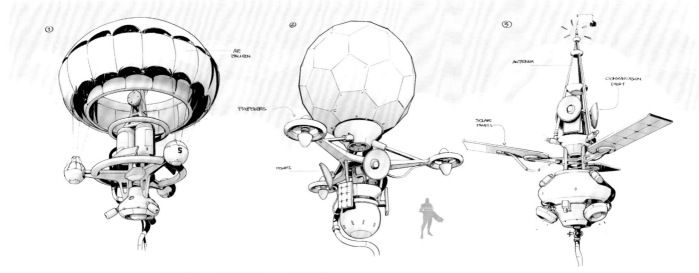

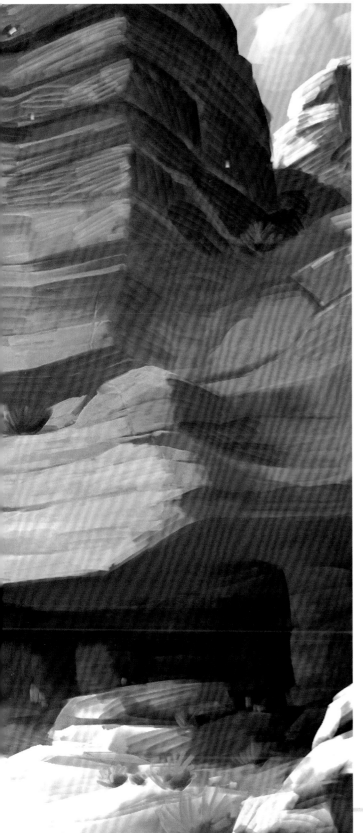

LEFT: **BEN ZHANG**; TOP: **OSCAR CAFARO**; BOTTOM LEFT: **AL CRUTCHLEY**

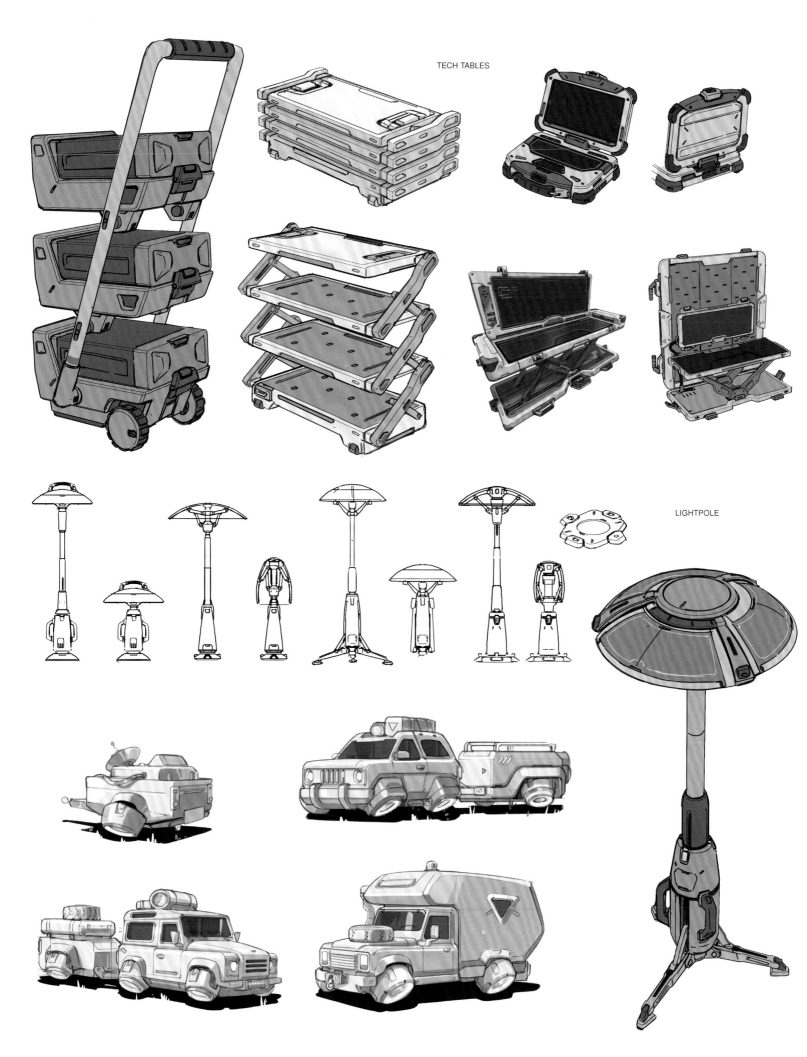

TECH TABLES

LIGHTPOLE

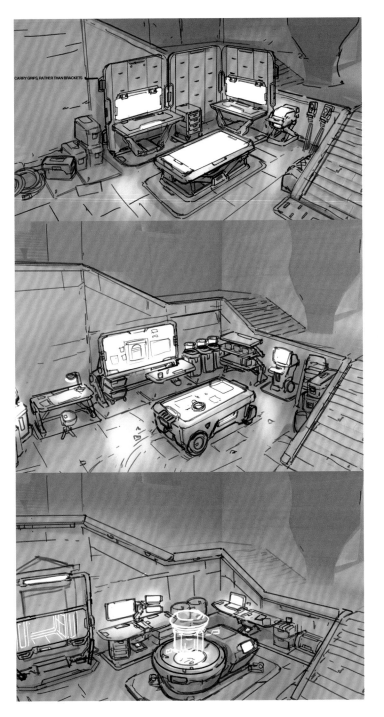

Artists concepted different versions of this group's equipment to convey as much detail as they could about how these archaeologists operate. The design emphasis was on portability, and many of the props feature wheels or joints that give the impression they could collapse into smaller objects.

"We made a point to say, when you're designing this stuff, imagine if only two people could carry it," said Rogers. "If it took more than two people, then this group wouldn't have that kind of equipment. So that's the idea behind the initial design of these props."

TENT CONCEPTS

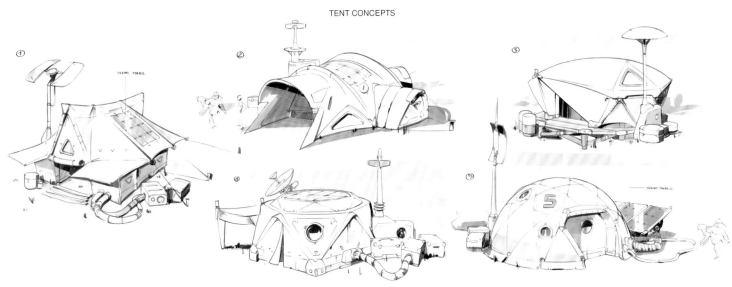

TOP LEFT: **AL CRUTCHLEY**; RIGHT AND BOTTOM: **OSCAR CAFARO**

BUSAN

Released on August 22, 2018, Busan is a prime example of the team's goal to create environments that have deep and meaningful ties to *Overwatch*'s heroes. The futuristic Korean city is home to one of the game's most popular characters, D.Va, and the designers found every opportunity they could to highlight this connection.

As with Junkertown, the map features three distinct areas that give players a sense of progression: the MEKA base, the futuristic city, and a traditional temple. The base, where D.Va and her fellow mech pilots are stationed, is a highly advanced military facility. The designers created many concepts of the location to capture the feeling that it is the pinnacle of technology.

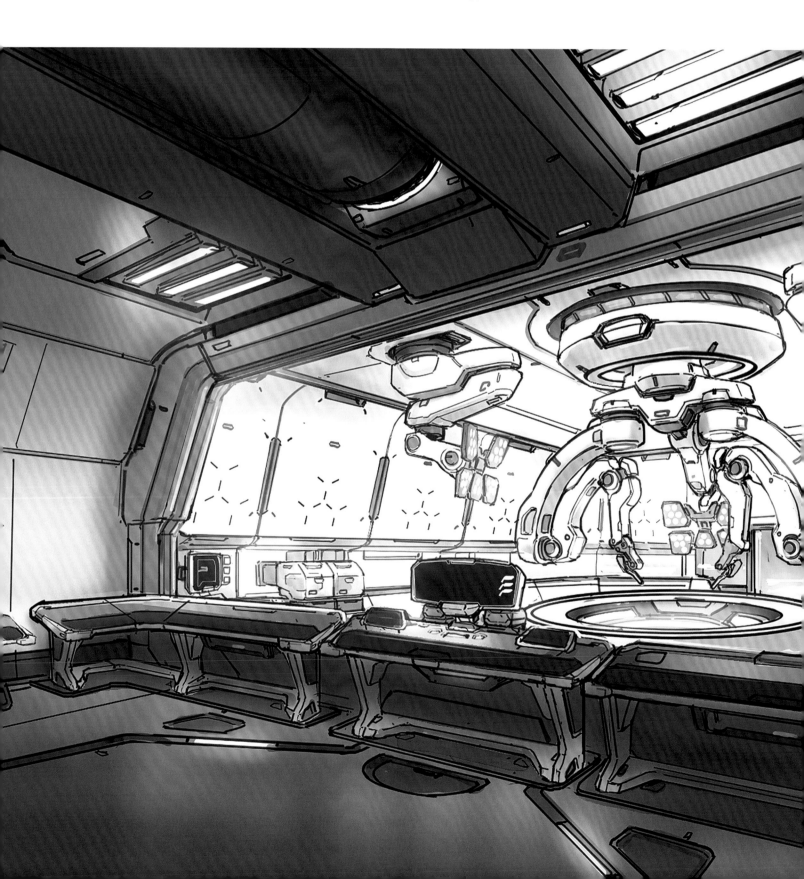

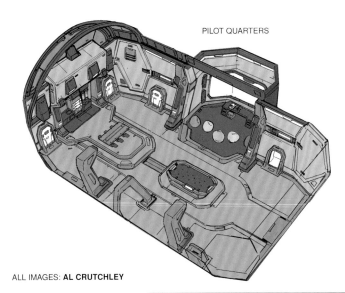

PILOT QUARTERS

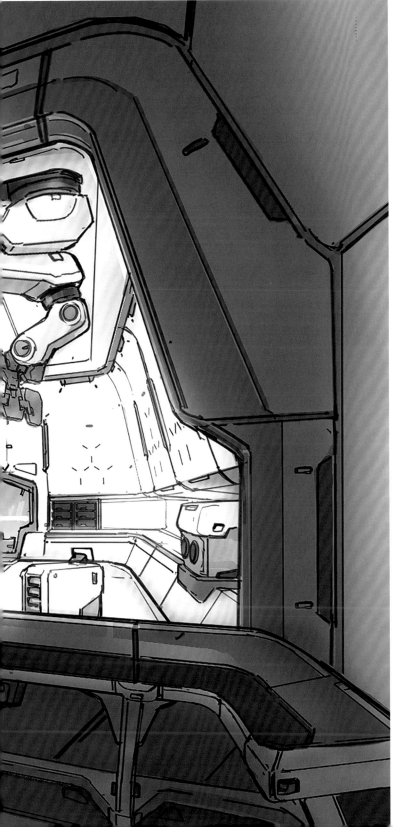

BEAST

SINGIJEON

YUNA

KYUNG-SOO

La Princesse

MASTERMIND

JAE-EUN

SEUNG-HWA

ALL IMAGES: **BEN ZHANG**

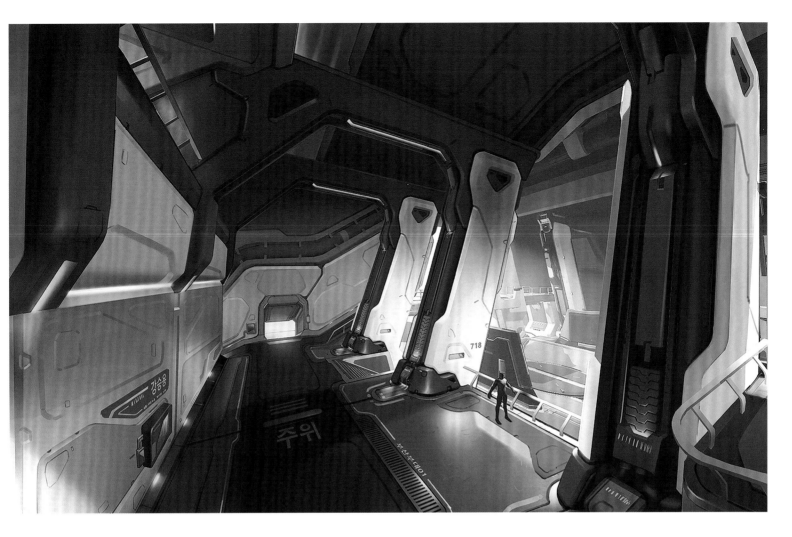

TOP: **DAVID KANG**; BOTTOM: **VASILI ZORIN**

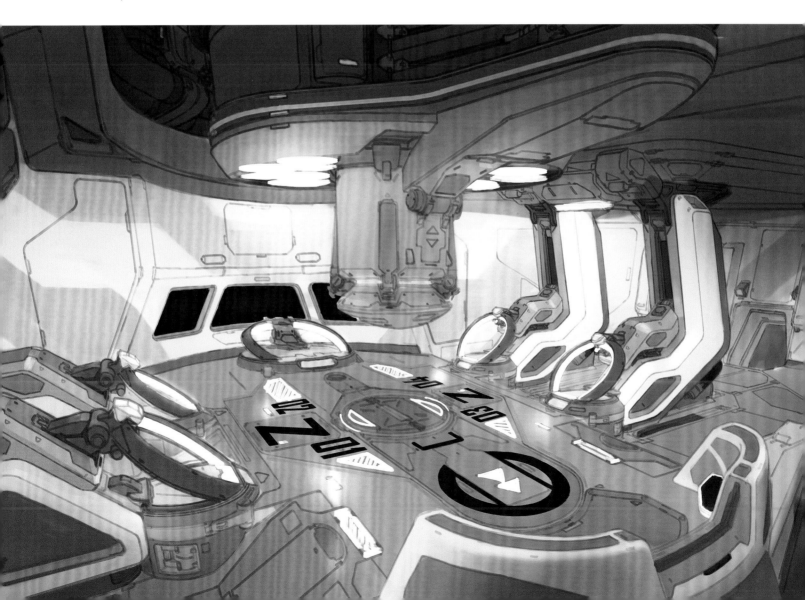

"We were very specific about the architecture and shapes for the design of the base," said senior environment artist Al Crutchley. "We couldn't say this was just general Overwatch tech, like the kind seen in Watchpoint: Gibraltar. It had to look distinct from other tech in *Overwatch*."

Artists also scattered hints of D.Va's presence and daily life throughout the base, creating everything from the hero's dorm room to stations where she and the other mech pilots do simulated training. Early concept art featured a common area with a huge entertainment screen where the MEKA crew could play games and hang out on their down time. Some of the elements in this room were later simplified and scaled down.

For the area of the map that features Busan itself, the designers wanted to honor what the city looks like but also give it futuristic touches. "We talked to people who lived there and people who had visited," said Rogers. "What are the iconic things that visitors notice in the city?"

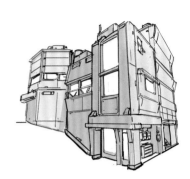

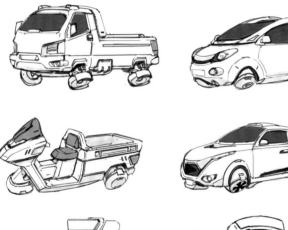
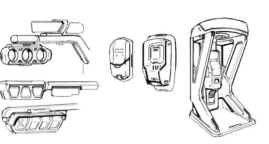

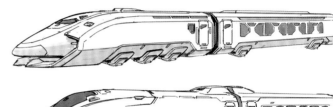
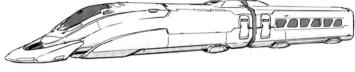
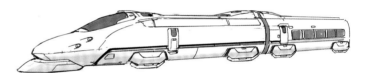
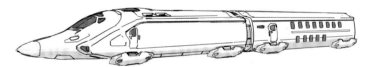

STOREFRONT CONCEPTS

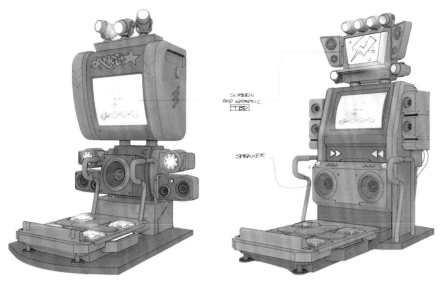

Karaoke establishments were reported among the familiar aspects of city life in Busan. The team put a spawn zone in one of them and even recorded special voice lines for heroes to sing before matches started.

When it came time to design the temple, artists preserved as much of the traditional aesthetic as possible. They added slight hints of technology to lanterns and other parts of the architecture, but not so much that it diluted the contrast with the more futuristic parts of the map.

KARAOKE BAR CONCEPTS

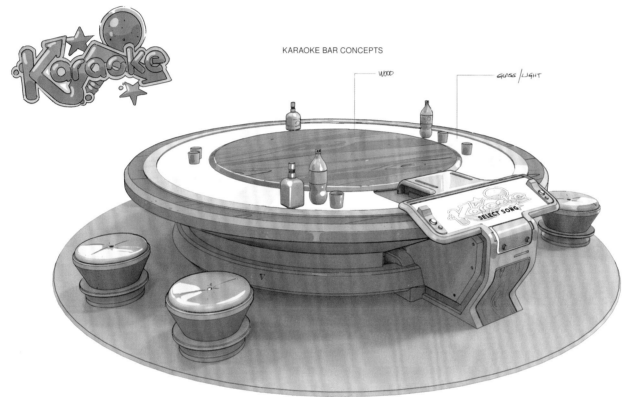

WOOD

GLASS/LIGHT

SELECT SONG

TOP: **OSCAR CAFARO**; BOTTOM: **DAVID KANG**

부산건물

PARIS

The designers had always wanted to make Paris. It was one of those cities that played perfectly into their goal to make *Overwatch* a game where players could visit famous locations around the world. On January 30, 2019, the team delivered on that fantasy.

But reaching that point required the designers to explore many different versions of Paris. A relatively quick way to visualize and review ideas for the map was by creating illustrations called mood pieces. These helped the team decide the correct tone for the environment. Some of the early concepts were too fantastical and stylized, but they gave the designers ideas for what to do next.

"Things that stood out were all Art Nouveau architecture," said associate art director Dion Rogers. "We tried to advance it eighty years, but still use it heavily throughout the map. We wanted to respect the original architecture and make the world feel relatable to people."

TOP: **AL CRUTCHLEY**; BOTTOM: **PATRICK FAULWETTER**

This philosophy of keeping things relatable extended to the Eiffel Tower. "This was a chance to add some sci-fi elements to the famous landmark," said Rogers. The team's early concepts envisioned the tower as highly stylized. Gradually, the designers brought it a bit closer to the real-life version. They added futuristic lighting to parts of the Eiffel Tower to give it a sci-fi touch while keeping it recognizable.

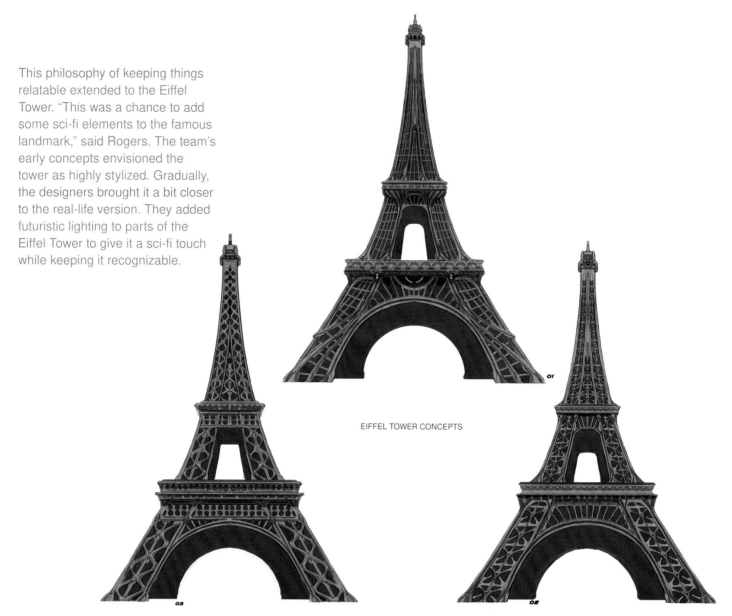

EIFFEL TOWER CONCEPTS

FACADE CONCEPTS

TOP: **AL CRUTCHLEY**; BOTTOM: **YEWON PARK**

WATERCRAFT CONCEPTS

WATER TAXI CONCEPTS

TOP: **OSCAR CAFARO**; BOTTOM: **LAURENT PIERLOT**

MOPED CONCEPTS

CITROËN VAN CONCEPTS

TOP, MIDDLE LEFT, AND BOTTOM: **OSCAR CAFARO**; MIDDLE RIGHT: **MATHIAS VERHASSELT**

LIGHT FIXTURE CONCEPTS

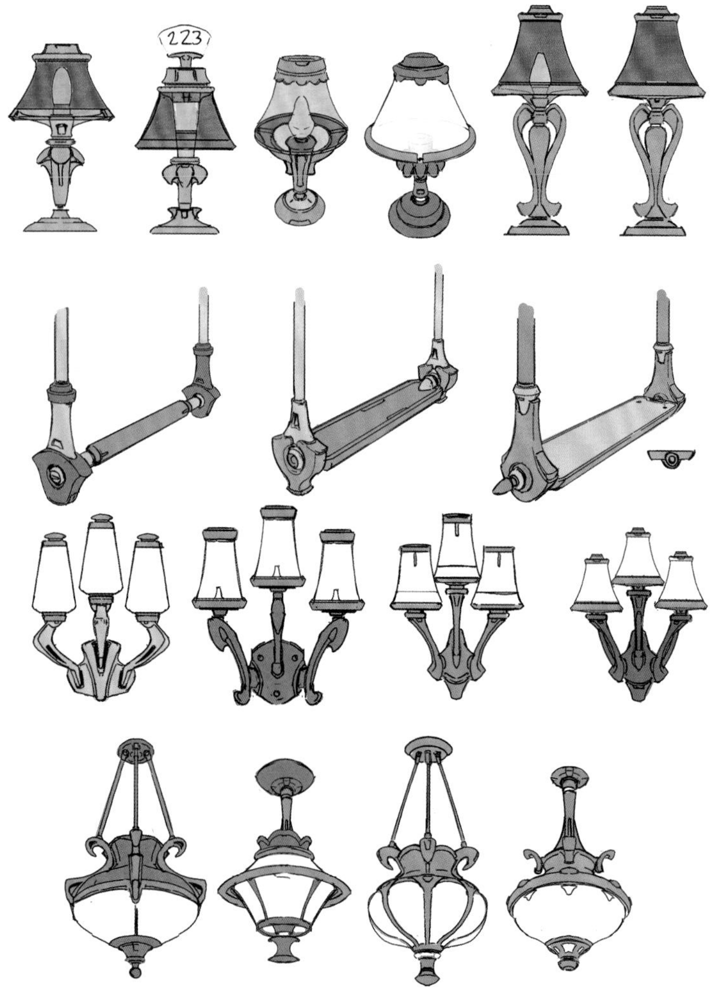

223

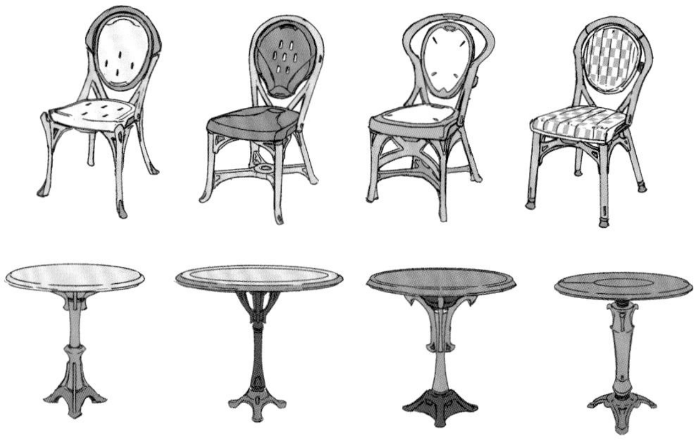

PLANTERS

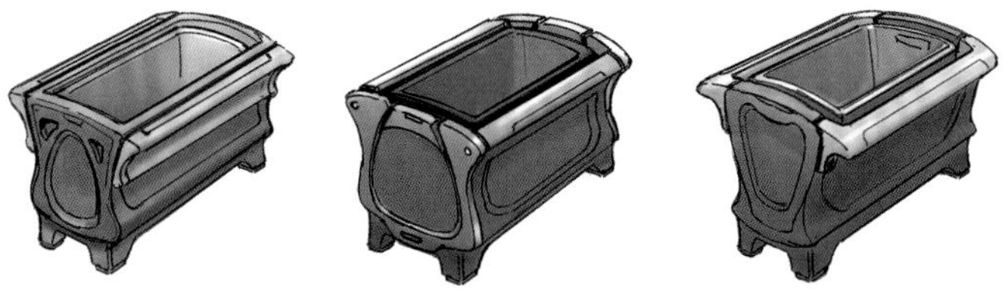

KIOSK

JEUDI
19°
12°

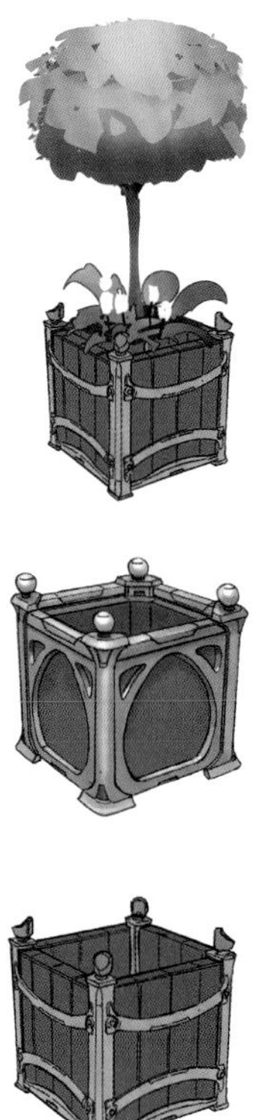

TOP: **AL CRUTCHLEY**; BOTTOM LEFT: **OSCAR CAFARO**

LUNA CABARET POSTERS

OMNIC SINGER

▶ **CABARET SPAWN ROOM** —Spawn rooms are important parts of every map. They give the designers an opportunity to set the mood of the environment. They are also the perfect place to layer in story elements that might go unnoticed in other areas of the map once battle is underway. For Paris, the cabaret spawn room offered another opportunity: a chance to test how players might interact with NPCs in *Overwatch 2*. The designers created a cabaret singer—named after concept artist Llia Yu's cat, Luna—who would sing and make comments to the heroes.

TOP AND RIGHT: **LLIA YU**; BOTTOM LEFT: **AQUATIC MOON**

HAVANA

With its colorful buildings, classic cars, and beautiful neoclassical architecture, Havana was a perfect candidate for bringing into the Overwatch world. The only question was when the right time would be to introduce it. The team found an opportunity with the Storm Rising Archives event beginning on April 16, 2019. Following the example of Rialto, the team made two variations of the map: one for the PVE mission and one for PVP gameplay.

"For the PVE mission, we wanted to have a storm rolling into Havana. We were testing out how weather can impact the environment. That storm made it more real—a living and breathing place," said senior art director Bill Petras. "The value of a dynamic world was important." Lead technical artist Lan-Fang Chang had previously experimented with a giant sandstorm rolling through the Temple of Anubis map, which ultimately helped the team create a hurricane in Havana. There were technical challenges to overcome as well as artistic ones. Havana is a vibrant place, and the designers didn't want the storm to mute its colors. As a solution, they started the PVE mission off with a beautiful sunny day.

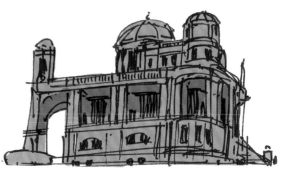

TOP: **OSCAR CAFARO**; BOTTOM: **PATRICK FAULWETTER**

"That gave it a familiar look. The storm is on the horizon, and as you go through the map, it gets closer," said Rogers. "We didn't want to make a map that was in dark hurricane weather the whole time. We transitioned from a sunny day to a storm—and that allowed us to maintain the aspirational version of the city."

Because the mission in Storm Rising follows a linear progression—sending players from one end of the map to the other—the designers had full control over how and when the hurricane would descend on the city. That wasn't the case for the PVP map, where players have more freedom to move about as they please. The team ultimately decided to remove the storm element completely from PVP, keeping the weather bright and sunny to highlight the colorful beauty of the seaside city.

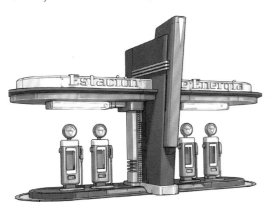
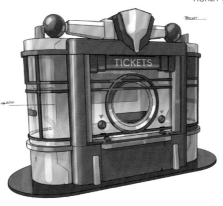

TICKET BOOTH

TOP: **LLIA YU**; MIDDLE AND BOTTOM: **OSCAR CAFARO**

TOP: **DAVID KANG**; MIDDLE AND BOTTOM: **PATRICK FAULWETTER**

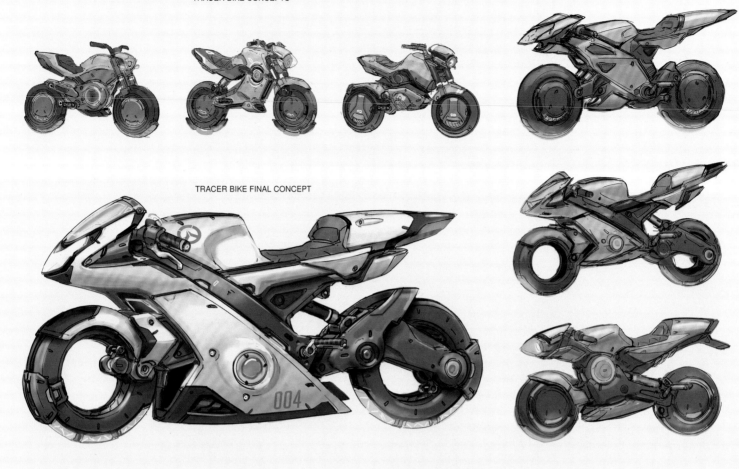

TRACER BIKE CONCEPTS

TRACER BIKE FINAL CONCEPT

PAYLOAD CONCEPTS

TOP: **AL CRUTCHLEY** AND **PATRICK FAULWETTER**; BOTTOM: **OSCAR CAFARIO**

HAVANA CAR CONCEPTS

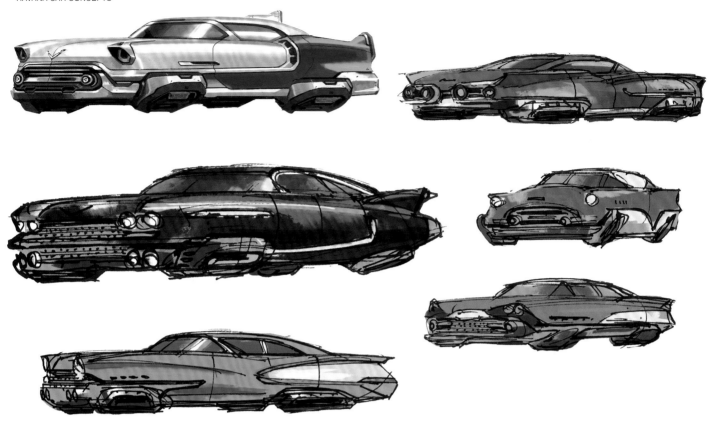

MAXIMILIEN CAR CONCEPTS

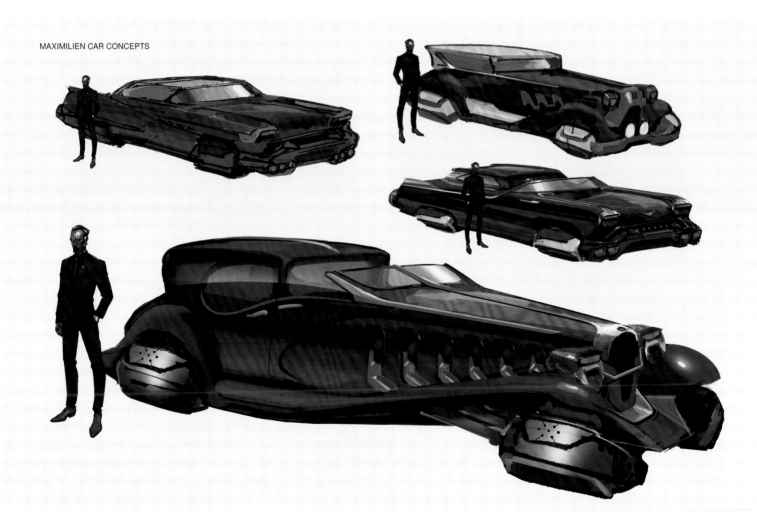

TOP: **OSCAR CAFARO**; MIDDLE AND BOTTOM: **PATRICK FAULWETTER**

POSTER IDEATION

POSTER ART

TOP: **REBECCA CHAN**; MIDDLE: **NATE BOWDEN**; BOTTOM RIGHT: **AQUATIC MOON**

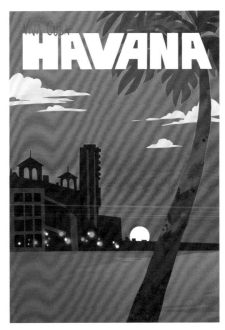

TOP LEFT AND BOTTOM MIDDLE: **GLEN BROGAN** FOR **HERO COMPLEX GALLERY**; TOP RIGHT AND BOTTOM LEFT: **REBECCA CHAN**

BLACK FOREST

After the game launched, the *Overwatch* team released a number of arena maps—smaller locations made for 4 vs. 4 or 3 vs. 3 game modes. Black Forest, Castillo, and Necropolis fell into this category, all released on May 23, 2017.

Months before Black Forest was made available, the team had put out another map set in Germany. Eichenwalde featured an abandoned village at the foot of a beautiful, medieval-style castle. The environment was closely tied to Reinhardt and his backstory—the hero had fought in a brutal battle there during the Omnic Crisis.

For Black Forest, the designers wanted to draw on many of

the same geographical themes as Eichenwalde but focus more on the surrounding woodlands. "The goal was to make a green map—a forest with a lot of vegetation," said associate art director Dion Rogers. "But that is difficult to do in a first-person shooter, because players can shoot through foliage. Could we pull off a version that works with *Overwatch*'s gameplay and intense hero combat?"

To address these concerns, the team included large trees with big trunks, which players could use as cover. Instead of creating bushes and other undergrowth, the designers layered dead leaves and mulch on the ground to give the impression of a damp, earthy forest.

MILL IDEATIONS

▶ **OMNIC CRISIS DEBRIS** — Black Forest is littered with the detritus of war, echoes of a battle that raged between omnics and humans in years past. These elements add more visual points of interest to go along with the overgrown buildings and dense forest, but they also flesh out more backstory for the Omnic Crisis and the style of technology that existed at the time.

The team created different versions of drop pods that had once crash-landed in the forest and released Bastion units. Some were enormous. Others were small. "We had a lot of freedom to explore," said senior environment artist Al Crutchley. "The smaller one ended up being the final version. We wanted something small that players could walk across."

TOP: **AL CRUTCHLEY**

CASTILLO

Using an approach similar to Black Forest, the team also released Castillo on May 23, 2017. The map has strong ties to Dorado, an existing environment set in Mexico. Although the two locations share visual themes, the designers created entirely new assets and a layout for Castillo.

"We used the existing look and feel of Dorado, which was very helpful," said Rogers. "That set the tone for us. The challenge was just creating more of it."

Beyond the aesthetic, the designers wanted to connect Castillo to Dorado from a lore standpoint. Dorado had introduced concepts like the Los Muertos gang and towering pyramid-like power plants belonging to the LumériCo energy company. Castillo added another layer to these elements by featuring both a statue of LumériCo's founder and a Los Muertos lair, scrawled with their distinct luminescent graffiti.

But Castillo did more than just build on Dorado's story; it blazed its own trail. The designers built Sombra's hideout

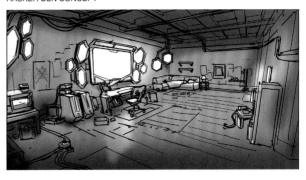

into the map, right down to a table strewn with tools and the hacker's disassembled translocator. Dossiers of familiar faces—all former Overwatch agents—litter the room. Every detail says something about who Sombra is, from her mastery of technology to her favorite hobby: collecting information on powerful individuals.

McCree's presence is also hinted at in the map: his hat is featured on a bar counter. The inspiration for this came from the *Reflections* comic, released in December of 2016, which

showed the hero had visited the location. A map belonging to Junkrat and Roadhog—along with one of the latter's gas canisters—lies on a table in the same location, implying that the two Junkers passed through the area at some point to perform a heist.

TOP: **AL CRUTCHLEY**

ENVIRONMENTS
NECROPOLIS

Like its predecessors, Necropolis is thematically linked to an existing map: Temple of Anubis. "That was a dear location to the artists on the team. The question was, how do we add lore to the space?" said associate art director Dion Rogers.

Ana—the first character released postlaunch—is from Egypt. In *Overwatch*'s story, she is presumed dead and in hiding. Necropolis seemed like a fitting place to highlight that lore.

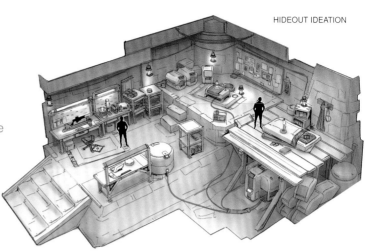

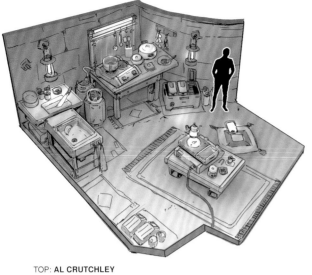

"It was fun to come up with," said Rogers. "She's been living here for a few years. But what did she do to the area, you know? You can see in the artwork that Ana has makeshift equipment lying around."

This equipment includes machines Ana could use to make her healing grenades, ammo, and sleep darts. Designers also included a bag belonging to Soldier: 76, hinting that he sought help from Ana at some time in the past. This encounter between the two heroes is elaborated on in the "Bastet" short story, which features illustrations set within the Necropolis.

TOP: **AL CRUTCHLEY**

CHÂTEAU GUILLARD

On August 29, 2017, the team released Château Guillard, a deathmatch game-mode map that highlighted Widowmaker's backstory. "It was the estate of the influential Guillard family—Widowmaker's ancestors," said Rogers. "It gradually fell into disrepair after the family's power waned during the French Revolution."

The designers envisioned that Widowmaker had taken ownership of the estate, using it as a hideout in between her missions.

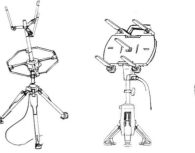

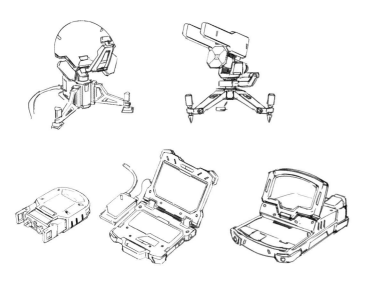

The surrounding lake was important for two reasons. First, it conveyed the fantasy of a remote and difficult to reach location—the perfect place for Widowmaker to lie low and plan her next move. Second, the lake created a barrier for the map, which was an organic way to define where players could and could not go. The team sprinkled small bits of lore throughout Château Guillard, from a wedding photo of Widowmaker and her late husband, Gérard Lacroix, to a sniper rifle case bearing the letter *W*. For the latter, artists concepted different versions to capture the right dimensions and level of detail.

TOP: **AL CRUTCHLEY**

KANEZAKA

One of the original maps released with *Overwatch* was Hanamura, a gorgeous Japanese town that features Genji and Hanzo's ancestral home, Shimada Castle. On January 12, 2021, the team invited players to experience the sights and sounds of Japan again with Kanezaka.

"The idea for the map was to expand on the city area of Hanamura since many people on the team felt that it's a really interesting part of the map that doesn't get as much playtime,"

said *Overwatch*'s senior level designer Morten Hedegren. "We also wanted to make sure that Kanezaka still felt connected to Hanamura, so we added the tower in the center; it shares some similarities with the temple areas in Hanamura. You can actually look up at Hanamura when playing Kanezaka."

Like Hanamura, Kanezaka explores the contrast between the country's traditional and futuristic architecture. Designers constructed the new deathmatch map with a mix of modern

high-rises and city streets bordered by older wooden buildings and a Buddhist tower. The general look of these sites was inspired by Gion, a historical district of Japan's ancient capital: Kyoto.

"Having visited Japan recently, the memories were still fresh in my mind. The sounds, the smells, the sights," said senior artist Thiago Klafke. "I tried to do those amazing memories justice so players can be transported to Japan while playing the map."

Despite the thematic similarities with Hanamura, the layout of Kanezaka is radically different from its predecessor. The developers carefully planned out the needs of a deathmatch map and applied them to Kanezaka. "We wanted to try and have lots of buildings where players could dodge in and out of as well as rooftops that provide vertical choices for the players—all while still making sure that it felt authentic to Japan," said Hedegren.

The diverse structures and visual themes were also used to help players familiarize themselves with the layout. "We discovered from older maps that players learn the space better when there are points of interest that are clearly different from each other. Even in a small space like a deathmatch map—it's important to create strong points of interest that players can use to navigate the battle," said Rogers. "The center shrine represents the middle of the map. You can orient yourself based on that."

Throughout Kanezaka's blend of old and new structures, the designers layered in subtle effects to create the feeling of a dynamic world. Sparks shoot from wiring in the narrow alleys, and steam drifts from heaters attached to the buildings. "At one point, there were fireflies everywhere, but the city looked like it was on fire. The fireflies felt like embers," said Rogers. "We changed it so that the fireflies were just under a bridge instead. That allowed the location to be a point of interest too."

▶ **DETAILS FROM HOME** — Apart from real-world inspirations, the team also packed Kanezaka with subtle details. The portraits in the cat café are based on pets belonging to some of the team's members. The rotating corgi outside the pottery shop is inspired by a pet belonging to one of *Overwatch*'s UI designers.

Kanezaka was created during the COVID-19 pandemic when the team was working entirely from home. "It was designed, concepted, and built entirely while we were remote," said associate art director Dion Rogers. "We didn't make any concepts of Kanezaka while we were at the office. This was a good moment for us. We discovered we can build something remotely, from start to finish."

LEFT AND TOP: **PETER LEE**; BOTTOM RIGHT: **ANDREW MENJIVAR**

NESSKAIN

SEASONAL EVENTS

After its release, *Overwatch* attracted a huge international following. Millions of players were logging in to battle it out as Tracer, Reaper, Bastion, and other heroes. Kaplan and the other designers knew they were living through a rare and special moment; they wanted to ride the wave they had caught and keep players engaged in this exciting new world with the introduction of seasonal events like Halloween Terror and Lunar New Year.

Each event was an enormous undertaking; the entire team and outside talent collaborated to create everything from icons and skins to environments and unique animations. Throughout this process, the designers were always eager to find ways to acknowledge the diversity of *Overwatch*'s international community.

"Seasonal events in *Overwatch* are about making the game feel alive, but also making it feel relevant and timely to what's going on in the world. We want players to feel this connection between the game that they're playing and their real life. And that's part of what we hope the seasonal events can do for everyone," said *Overwatch*'s game director, Aaron Keller. "The best part of working on this team is how much it cares about inclusivity and representing other people."

SUMMER GAMES

The first Summer Games came out in 2016, shortly after *Overwatch*'s release. Once the event was over, the team discussed what to do the next year. Would they keep doing the same event or invent new ones every couple of months? Ultimately, they decided to make Summer Games an annual tradition.

"Initially, we were trying to celebrate the summer sports and all of the events that go on around summer. Summer is a time when people do a lot of outdoor activities. We wanted to capture that—we wanted to have a very cohesive idea to tie them all together," said principal game designer Michael Heiberg. "So that was the main theme initially. We had

SPRAYS

ALL IMAGES: **AQUATIC MOON**

these subthemes of summer get-togethers and barbeques that we explored a little more as time went on, just to try different themes. There's only so far you can go with sports before you think, 'How many more sports can we add?' We tweaked the theme a little over time to attack different angles of it."

ICONS AND SPRAYS —For icons and sprays, the designers tapped into ideas and themes that weren't always applicable to the other seasonal events. The Bicycle Kick, Goal Blossom, and Safe Hands designs were all themed around Lúcioball, which is specific to Summer Games.

ICONS

2017

BIKER

CRICKET

AUSTRALIA

TOP: **QIU FANG**; BOTTOM: **MORTEN SKAALVIK**

A SALT RIFLE

DIET Heal4

RAISE THE × STEAKS ×

76

A SALT RIFLE

76

A SALT RIFLE

G-76

ALL IMAGES: **ANH DANG**

TULUM

COTE D'AZUR

TOP: **BEN ZHANG**; BOTTOM: **QIU FANG**

LIFEGUARD

WINGED VICTORY

ALL IMAGES: **QIU FANG**

2018

GRIDIRONHARDT

CABANA

CATCHER

FASTBALL

ZENYATTA 94

TOP: **LIPAN LIU**; BOTTOM: **ANH DANG**

WAVERACER D.VA —Building on 2017's themes, the designers continued creating sports- and beach-related skins in 2018. As with most events, the team often ties multiple skins to the same concept—in this case, the Pitcher and Catcher skins for Zenyatta and Winston. Artists incorporated elements from each character's lore into the designs, such as the Iris and Horizon Lunar Colony logos that feature on the heroes' uniforms.

WAVERACER

ARNOLD TSANG AND MORTEN SKAALVIK

LACROSSE

▶ **KENDOKA GENJI** — Many of the skins made in 2019 were themed around country flags and beachwear, but others were still inspired by international sports. Genji's 2019 skin is based on Japanese kendo. The designers wanted to give him a bamboo sword like those used in the martial art, but they had to keep it metal to preserve the hero's existing animations and effects. Ultimately, they found a creative way to incorporate the bamboo design into the skin by applying it to Genji's sheath.

WAVE

TOP LEFT: **DAVID KANG**; TOP RIGHT: **ARNOLD TSANG**; BOTTOM: **ANH DANG**

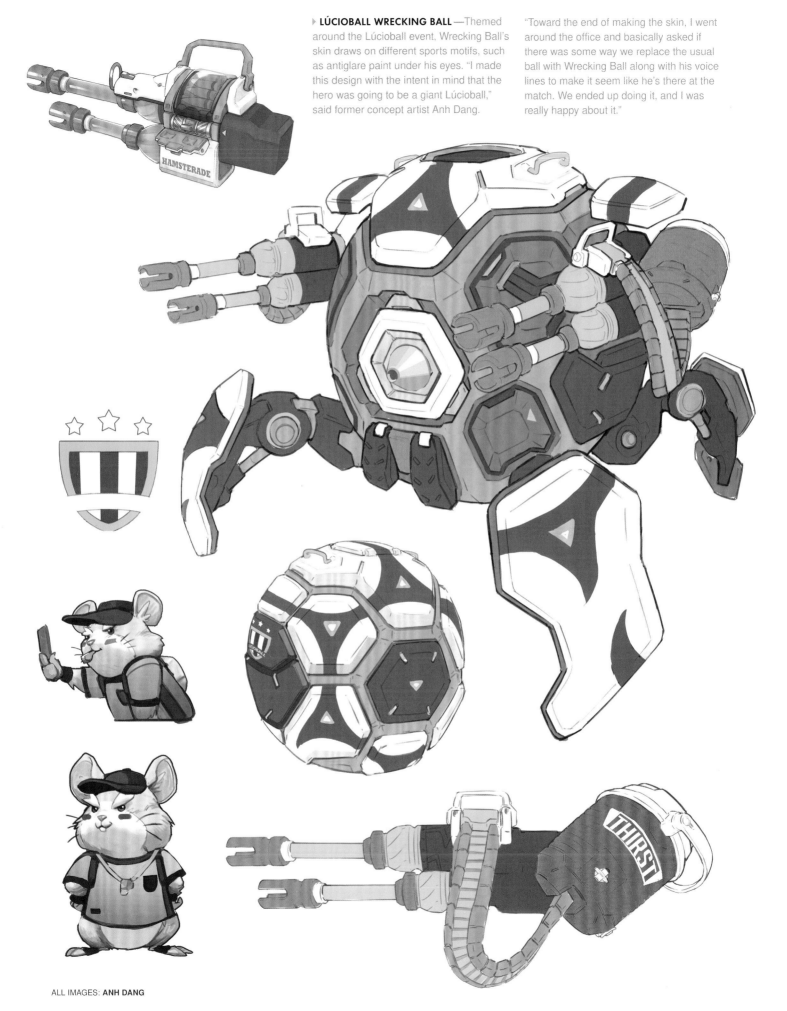

▶ **LÚCIOBALL WRECKING BALL**—Themed around the Lúcioball event, Wrecking Ball's skin draws on different sports motifs, such as antiglare paint under his eyes. "I made this design with the intent in mind that the hero was going to be a giant Lúcioball," said former concept artist Anh Dang.

"Toward the end of making the skin, I went around the office and basically asked if there was some way we replace the usual ball with Wrecking Ball along with his voice lines to make it seem like he's there at the match. We ended up doing it, and I was really happy about it."

ALL IMAGES: **ANH DANG**

DRIFTWOOD

REF FOR FISHES

FESKARN

▶ **SURF 'N' SPLASH TORBJÖRN** —Multiple explorations of Torbjörn's Surf 'N' Splash skin were made before finding the right look and feel. One of the earlier concepts featured the hero in floaties and adorned in nautical elements. "He actually has a pirate skin, so it felt a little too close to that one," said Dang, who concepted the skin. "I tried to lean more into the fun summer theme. He's at the beach, watching his grandchildren, playing with sandcastles and stuff."

TOP: **KEJUN WANG**; BOTTOM: **ANH DANG**

GUARD

▶ **LIFEGUARD PHARAH** — The idea for Pharah's Lifeguard skin was first inspired by water-powered jetpacks. "That in itself didn't feel like enough for the skin," said Tsang. "So we mixed in some lifeguard elements." Concept artist Daryl Tan melded the two themes together, creating water pipes that feed into Pharah's jetpack and giving her the iconic red-and-white lifeguard color scheme.

Creating this skin presented challenges due to Pharah's base appearance. "She was done more like an action figure. So her proportions were exaggerated, and she had longer limbs here and there. And every part of her body was armored up. The trick was finding the middle ground—we wanted to show more organic parts of her," said Tan. "That was something we had a lot of back-and-forth about with the 3-D modelers and riggers. Which parts do we have to have the armor on? For example, her thighs have to have missiles coming out of them."

▶ **LIFEGUARD PHARAH'S WEAPON** — "Because she's a lifeguard, we thought about making her weapon a flare gun. I combined that idea with those buoys that are out in the open sea—the whole front of the gun is like that," said Tan. "I added the little walkie-talkie on the side just to give it some extra flair."

ALL IMAGES: **DARYL TAN**

KARATE

SURF'S UP

TOP: **KEJUN WANG**; BOTTOM: **DAVID KANG**

▶ **TROPICAL BAPTISTE** —The release of more heroes gave the designers new characters to play with for each Summer Games event. Baptiste's Tropic skin was inspired by his Caribbean origins as well as previous lore released about the character. His shirt is based on the same outfit he wears in an illustration from the "What You Left Behind" short story.

ALL IMAGES: **MORTEN SKAALVIK**

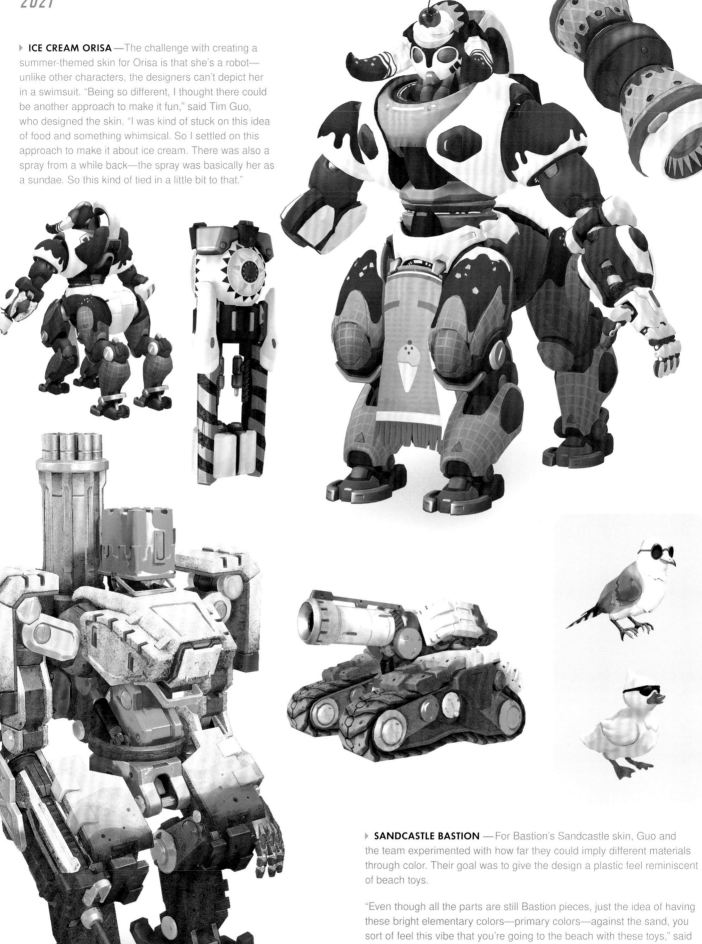

▶ **ICE CREAM ORISA**—The challenge with creating a summer-themed skin for Orisa is that she's a robot—unlike other characters, the designers can't depict her in a swimsuit. "Being so different, I thought there could be another approach to make it fun," said Tim Guo, who designed the skin. "I was kind of stuck on this idea of food and something whimsical. So I settled on this approach to make it about ice cream. There was also a spray from a while back—the spray was basically her as a sundae. So this kind of tied in a little bit to that."

▶ **SANDCASTLE BASTION** —For Bastion's Sandcastle skin, Guo and the team experimented with how far they could imply different materials through color. Their goal was to give the design a plastic feel reminiscent of beach toys.

"Even though all the parts are still Bastion pieces, just the idea of having these bright elementary colors—primary colors—against the sand, you sort of feel this vibe that you're going to the beach with these toys," said Guo. "The only thing that was a geometry change on this one was that his head became a bucket."

ALL IMAGES: **TIM GUO**

POOL PARTY

REFEREE

TOP LEFT: **KELVIN CHAN**; TOP RIGHT: **NATALIE PELLMAN**; BOTTOM: **YIMING LIU**

▶ **MERMAID SYMMETRA** —Always eager to push the limits of what was possible with skins, the team approached a new look for Symmetra in 2021 that proved to be technically challenging. The hero can only have a limited number of moving parts, such as her dress and her hair. "Those were already pushing the limits on the number of physics-based objects we can put on the character," said Tan. "So with this skin I was pushing it even further because my first pass had a lot more tail and mermaid fins all over the place."

In later versions, Tan adjusted the skin's mermaid-like features so they wouldn't require too much movement. "We just go back and forth until we get it working the way we want it to, but we are careful not to lose the integrity of the skin."

For Symmetra's weapon, Tan drew on elements from waves and sea creatures. Finding the right color was just as important as outfitting the hero's equipment with ocean-themed filigree. "I try to find a color that ties the weapon to her. Her gun would stand out from her, and she would stand out from the gun. It's important to keep the read of it as clear as possible."

RIO COURT

ALL IMAGES: **AL CRUTCHLEY**

▶ **LÚCIOBALL** —The 2016 Summer Games event featured Lúcioball, the first new game mode the Overwatch team had ever made. For 2017 and subsequent years, the designers continued the Lúcioball tradition, but they were always on the lookout for ways to enhance it.

"It wasn't until 2020 that we tried something a little more out there with it. We took an opportunity to make each of the arena maps different, depending on where the location is in the world. At the same time, we did an experiment on the side, where I just spawned in an extra ball," said principal game designer Michael Heiberg. "Then I spawned a few more . . . and then I spawned in a few dozen. I talked to the team and asked, 'What do you think?' And they said, 'We have to do this.' So then we made Lúcioball Remix. Combined with the new maps, I think we got a lot of fun gameplay out of that."

HALLOWEEN TERROR

The Halloween Terror event is a celebration of everything spooky and fun about Halloween. The unique holiday gives the team an opportunity to explore costumed and monster versions of characters that it doesn't have any other time of year. One of the key features of Halloween Terror is Junkenstein's Revenge, a PVE game mode that pits four players against the mad scientist Dr. Junkenstein and his monstrous cohorts.

Creating this game mode sprang from a desire to expand *Overwatch* beyond just PVP. "We were thinking it would be fun to try something that is PVE. And we were also wanting to learn more about making PVE content in general. It would be nice to explore some of that, but to take it one step at a time," said Michael Heiberg. "So the very first thing for us to try was a holdout-style game mode. From that, Junkenstein's Revenge was born."

SPRAYS

SPRAYS—The Trick or Treat sprays soon became a major focus for the designers, as they imagine the heroes in their younger days, dressed up as their *future* selves. For each one, artists try to find elements that evoke the character's personality or demeanor. For example, Ashe stealing candy, or Soldier: 76 dutifully (if not reluctantly) sitting outside his door to meet trick or treaters.

ONEMEGAWATT, QIU FANG, AQUATIC MOON, RAY COTTON, AND **ANH DANG**

"I kind of look at it as this made-up fantasy inside the Overwatch universe. It's supposed to be some sort of story that Reinhardt is telling," said *Overwatch*'s former lead writer, Michael Chu. "One of the interesting elements was figuring out the theme for the characters. It was fun to go, 'If we had this fantasy universe, what would be a cool version of each hero?'"

For 2017, one of these characters the team imagined as existing in the Junkenstein universe was Viking Torbjörn. The designers drew inspiration from Norse history to transform the engineer into a fierce warrior. The equipment on his back was reimagined as a giant Norse compass, and his claw was based off the mast of a Viking ship.

ICONS

▶ **JIANGSHI MEI** —The team often found inspiration for new skins in fascinating places, including Chinese vampire movies. The undead creatures in these films feature specific visual motifs: They are often dressed as magistrates, with a distinct heron embroidered on the chest. Yellow sheets of paper scrawled with runes can be stuck to their heads to prevent them from moving. "The backpack also has a Taoist monk symbol—they always defeat the vampires, and they're always dressed in yellow," said Tsang. "The eight-sided mirror wards off evil spirits."

To accompany the skin, the team also gave Mei a new emote based on the way that vampires in these films hop around with their arms outstretched.

VIKING

TOP: **MORTEN SKAALVIK**; BOTTOM: **HICHAM HABCHI**; RIGHT: **ANH DANG**

▶ **DRAGON SYMMETRA** —Symmetra's Dragon skin had been concepted before Halloween Terror. When the event came around, the team saw it as the perfect opportunity to unveil the new design and incorporate it into the Junkenstein's Revenge game mode. "This was one of the skins that former principal artist Laurel Austin did," said Tsang. "She always has brilliant ideas. The wings wrap around Symmetra like a dress. The place where she reloads—the circular opening—Laurel made it a dragon's eye. We were able to make it blink in-game."

CULTIST

TOP: **LAUREL AUSTIN**; BOTTOM: **MORTEN SKAALVIK**

DRACULA

TOTALLY '80S

TOP LEFT: **ARNOLD TSANG**; TOP RIGHT: **ANH DANG**; BOTTOM: **ROMAN KENNEY**

▶ **CORSAIR ANA** — Ana's Corsair skin reimagines the sniper as a rifle-toting privateer. In keeping with the maritime theme, the developers created a parrot to accompany the hero. Due to limited animation resources, they couldn't have the bird accompany Ana throughout gameplay, but they found creative ways to bring it into other aspects of the game. By reusing assets from Ganymede—Bastion's bird companion—the designers were able to showcase the parrot in Ana's Hero Select and victory poses.

VAN HELSING

ALL IMAGES: **HICHAM HABCHI**

▶ **SWAMP MONSTER DOOMFIST** — Doomfist's Swamp Monster is an homage to classic monster movies—the perfect type of skin to explore for the Halloween Terror event. The challenge of designing this skin lay in finding a balance in how much the hero's features could be changed.

"One of the tricky parts with making a character into another species is you need to keep the facial features in the exact same place, so you can't move the mouth or nose around to make it look like a different species. We did our best to make him look less human by cutting off his nose but keeping his nostrils in the same place," said concept artist David Kang, who designed the skin.

SLASHER: 76

TOP: **DAVID KANG**; BOTTOM: **MORTEN SKAALVIK**

▶ BANSHEE MOIRA —For many of the skins, the designers think up backstories to explain who these versions of the heroes are and where they come from. Banshee Moira was allegedly a princess from a nearby castle who died in the woods and became a menacing ghost. "We tried to come up with some ancient-feeling patterns, more Celtic designs because she's from that area," said concept artist Qiu Fang, who created the skin along with artist Ben Zhang. "So it feels like she's been haunting this area for millennia."

ENCHANTED ARMOR

TOP: **BEN ZHANG** AND **QIU FANG**; BOTTOM: **ANH DANG**

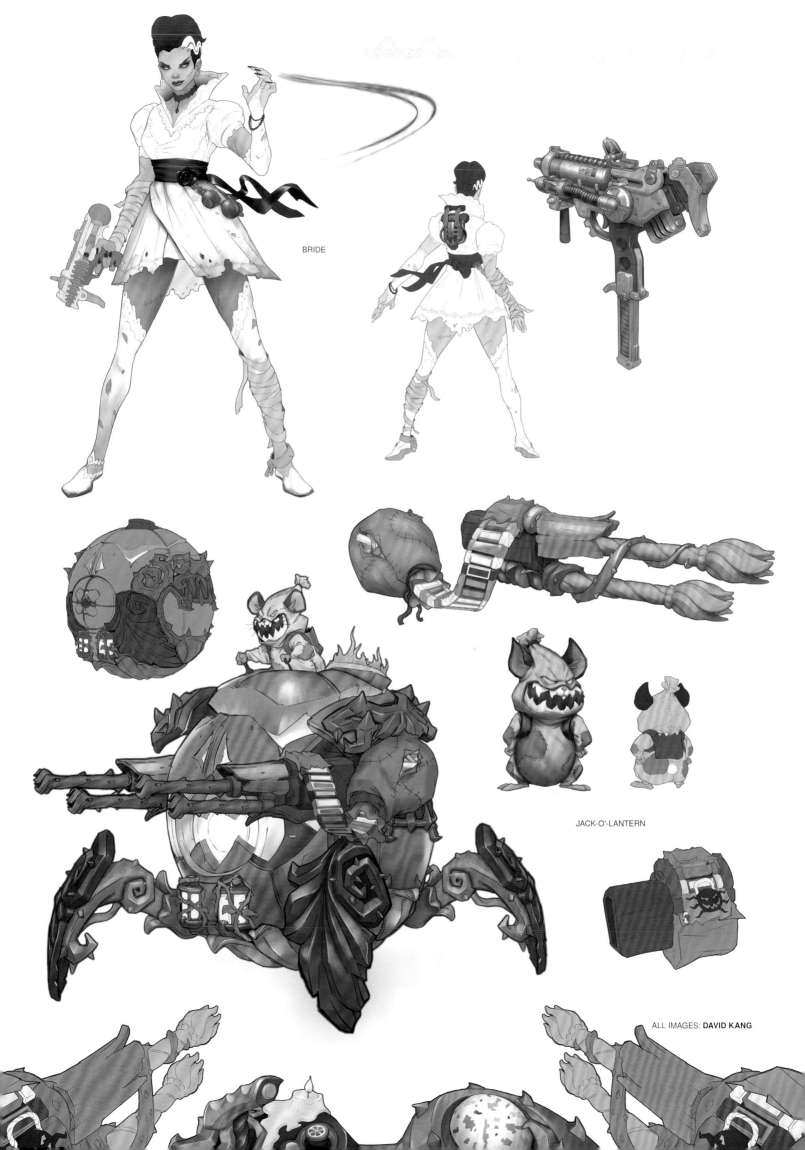

BRIDE

JACK-O'-LANTERN

ALL IMAGES: **DAVID KANG**

2019

DEMON

WARLOCK

TOP: **ANH DANG** AND **BEN ZHANG**; BOTTOM: **QIU FANG**; MIDDLE: **DARYL TAN**

WILL-O'-WISP

PHARAOH

TOP: **QIU FANG**; BOTTOM: **MORTEN SKAALVIK**

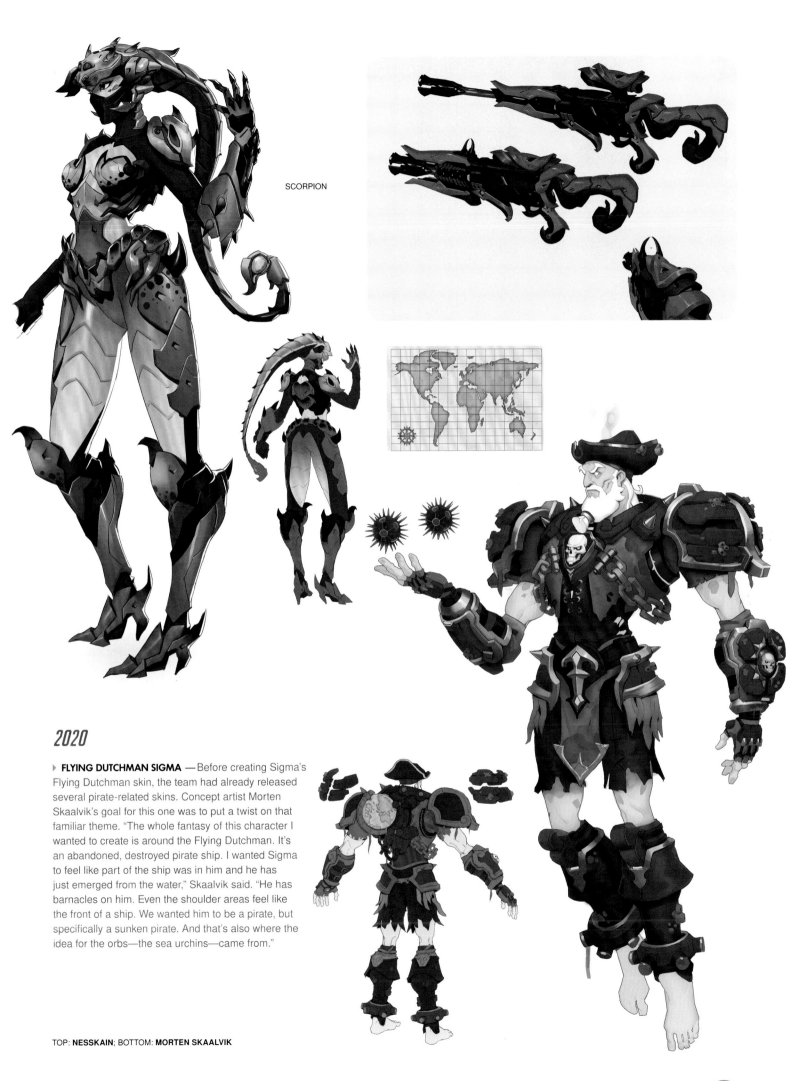

SCORPION

2020

▶ **FLYING DUTCHMAN SIGMA** —Before creating Sigma's Flying Dutchman skin, the team had already released several pirate-related skins. Concept artist Morten Skaalvik's goal for this one was to put a twist on that familiar theme. "The whole fantasy of this character I wanted to create is around the Flying Dutchman. It's an abandoned, destroyed pirate ship. I wanted Sigma to feel like part of the ship was in him and he has just emerged from the water," Skaalvik said. "He has barnacles on him. Even the shoulder areas feel like the front of a ship. We wanted him to be a pirate, but specifically a sunken pirate. And that's also where the idea for the orbs—the sea urchins—came from."

TOP: **NESSKAIN**; BOTTOM: **MORTEN SKAALVIK**

▶ **DAI-TENGU HANZO AND KARASU-TENGU GENJI** —Concept artist Kejun Wang worked on both the Karasu-Tengu Genji and Dai-Tengu Hanzo skins together in order to create a unified theme between them. "Usually there are two types of tengus," said Wang, referring to a type of creature in Japanese folklore. "One has a long nose. The other is like a crow. They're both from the same theme, but I wanted to make them look different. So I had more cloth and the traditional long nose for the Hanzo skin. It's more inspired by traditional Japanese costume. For Genji's skin, it's more crow inspired. I also wanted to choose very different colors so you can tell the difference between them right away."

Wang originally wanted to attach wings to their backs as well, but after discussing the concept with some of the team's tech artists, he discovered that adding these appendages to the characters' models might change their silhouettes and create animation issues. Rather than abandon the idea, he incorporated wing elements into Hanzo's feathery shoulder pad. Genji's weapons also draw on this idea: his sword has a feather motif, and the points of his shuriken resemble talons.

鴉

▶ **WEREWOLF WINSTON** —The team had always wanted
to do a skin based off a werewolf, one of the most iconic
horror movie monsters. The question was, which of the
existing heroes would be the best fit? "Winston was
probably one of the only characters we could give an
actual wolf face to," said Skaalvik, who created the skin.
"We ended up giving it a small twist of forest-related
elements, so it almost has a lumberjack feel to it."

This choice to pursue a woodland theme also helped
Skaalvik and the team find a solution for Winston's
jetpack. To make sure the skin matches the hero's
silhouette, abilities, and animations, they needed
something with a hard surface to replace his existing
equipment. Trees satisfied that need and also played into
the forest motif.

ALL IMAGES: **MORTEN SKAALVIK**

▶ **SHIN-RYEONG D.VA** — In different countries, there are variations on a classic folktale of a beautiful woman who can turn into a nine-tailed fox in order to consume the hearts of her lovers. Concept artist David Kang used these stories as inspiration to create D.Va's skin. "We tried to go a different route and lean on the side of her being evil and scary because this one is a Halloween Terror skin. I thought that was a fresh take on the nine-tail idea."

The designers had to overcome one major hurdle with this concept, though: the limited amount of polygons they can use on characters. "We actually have more polygons on the pilot in this skin than the base skin," said Kang. "This one has extra polygons for her dress, her ears, and her bandages." When character artists began modeling the skin, they found creative ways to take polygons away from the mech and add it to D.Va as a way to accommodate for the extra details.

Another challenge was depicting the skin's tails in a way that wouldn't create technical issues, such as clipping through D.Va, parts of the environment, or other characters. "We decided to convert her tails from physical to transparent, kind of magical in a way," said former lead character artist Renaud Garland. "So even if they clip through something, they disappear, and it feels okay."

ALL IMAGES: **DAVID KANG**

WINTER WONDERLAND

Much like Halloween Terror, Winter Wonderland embraced familiar colors, sights, and cultural festivities around the month of December. However, the intention was never to center this event around one specific holiday, such as Christmas. As with all of *Overwatch*'s events, the team wanted to make it feel international.

"There are many different types of cosmetic content in the game: skins, sprays, voice lines, and emotes. There are examples of every one of those that represent different cultures, areas of the world, values, and points of view," said Aaron Keller.

SPRAYS

AQUATIC MOON AND **JANICE CHU**

One example of this is Junkrat's Beachrat skin. "It's summer in Australia when it's winter in the northern hemisphere," said Tsang. "The skin seemed like a fun way to acknowledge that."

2017

SNOW OWL

RIME

SNOW WATCH

TOP: **MORTEN SKAALVIK**; BOTTOM LEFT: **ANH DANG**; BOTTOM RIGHT: **BEN ZHANG** AND **HICHAM HABCHI**

CASUAL

ALPINE: 76

ARTIC-169

76

TOP: **HICHAM HABCHI**; BOTTOM: **MORTEN SKAALVIK**

ICE FISHERMAN

TUNA

BEACHRAT

POP A ROO

TOP: **MORTEN SKAALVIK**; BOTTOM: **ANH DANG**

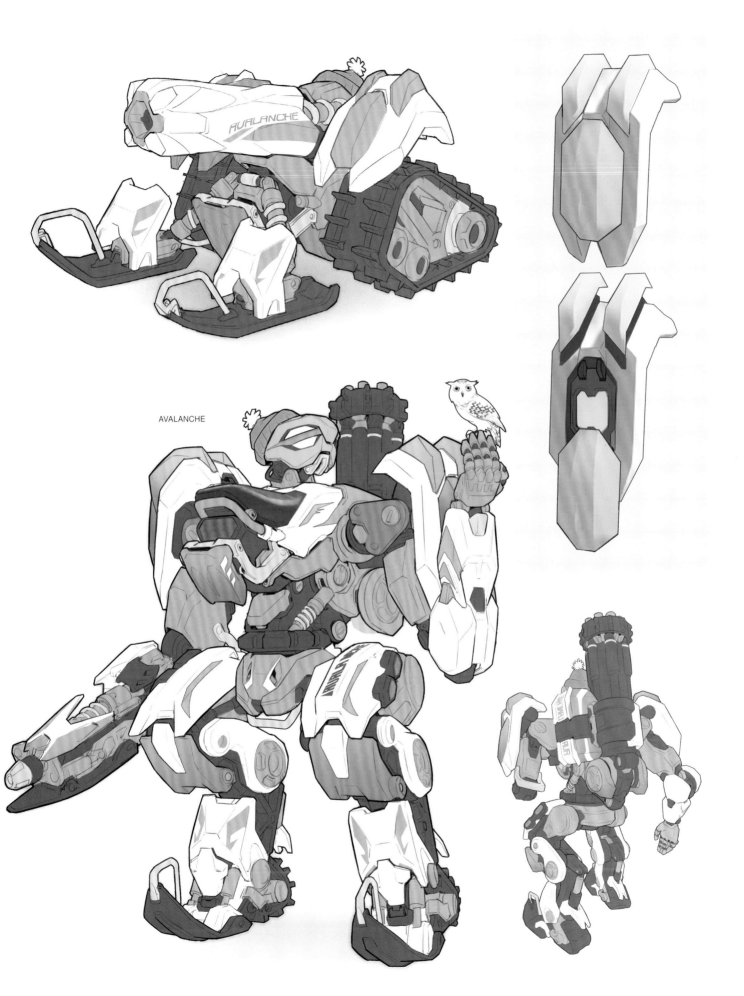

AVALANCHE

▶ **KRAMPUS JUNKRAT** —Another unique take came in the form of the Krampus Junkrat skin, a darker side to the winter holiday season. It was inspired by the folklore of Krampus, a goatlike demonic figure that punishes naughty children. Junkrat's unique physiology allowed the designers to explore this mythological figure in ways they wouldn't have been able to with other heroes. Specifically, they were able to mimic Krampus's goatlike reverse knee with Junkrat's peg leg.

SNOWBOARDER

TOP: **MORTEN SKAALVIK**; BOTTOM: **ANH DANG**

SNOW FOX

SUGAR PLUM FAIRY

TOP: **BEN ZHANG**; BOTTOM: **QIU FANG**

FIGURE SKATER

▶ **YETI HUNT** — Winter Wonderland was another opportunity for the team to create a new game mode. "We had tons of different ideas. One of the designers wanted to try a snowball fight—a one-shot kill mode," said principal game designer Michael Heiberg. "That kind of mode was interesting, and we thought we could make something playful that was also a little hardcore. But we found that it was a bit too challenging at first, so in later years we tried more casual modes. In 2017, we brought in the Yeti Hunt, which was our first asynchronous mode."

Yeti Hunt pitted five people playing as Mei in her Yeti Hunter skin against a single person assuming the role of Winston in his Yeti skin. To kick off the start of this new game mode, the team released a short comic—Yeti Hunt—written by Robert Brooks and illustrated by community artist Nathan "onemegawatt" Nguyen.

Hiver

BIATHALON

ALL IMAGES: **MORTEN SKAALVIK**

YETI HUNT.

ALL IMAGES: **ONEMEGAWATT**

RIME

▶ **RAT KING REAPER**—A recurring skin theme for Winter Wonderland is characters based on the famous Nutcracker ballet. Previously, the designers had created a skin for Zenyatta based around the Nutcracker character. For 2019, they reimagined Mercy as the Sugar Plum Fairy. The following year, they went for a more serious tone with the Rat King character. The original plan was to make the skin for Junkrat, but they decided Reaper would be a better fit, to give it a more villainous edge.

ALL IMAGES: **MORTEN SKAALVIK**

MOUNTAIN MAN

JÖTUNN

TOP: **DAVID KANG**; BOTTOM: **MORTEN SKAALVIK**

▶ **PENGUIN MEI** — For 2020, concept artist Kejun Wang brainstormed multiple ideas for a Mei skin before landing on the Penguin concept. "I felt like it actually matched her personality—just very cute combined with the Antarctic theme," he said. "The base character already had a winter-wear vibe. I think this animal feel really helped give her another visual hook."

Initially, Wang's concepts were more evocative of someone in an animal costume. "Like what people wear outside a store, handing out flyers. It was maybe too goofy, so I brought some tech elements into it to make it more sci-fi."

TOYBOT

TOP: **KEJUN WANG**; BOTTOM: **YIMING LIU**

LUMBERJACK

ALL IMAGES: **ARMANDO GONZALEZ-DORTA**

CONDUCTOR

ICE EMPRESS

99705

LEFT: **QIU FANG**; RIGHT: **YIMING LIU**

2020 EPIC SKINS

HOLLY

SNOW ANGEL

UGLY SWEATER: 76

ALL IMAGES: **MORTEN SKAALVIK**

LUNAR NEW YEAR

Lunar New Year is a massive holiday around the world, and one celebrated by many members of the *Overwatch* team. As with other events, releasing content around this holiday was an opportunity to connect with the game's international community.

"It's a chance to do sprays and other things that are exciting for our East Asian fans," said Tsang. "When we celebrate an event important to them, they appreciate that."

For Lunar New Year content, the designers create a cohesive theme to tie the event's various skins together. In 2017, they crafted the first of these sets by reimagining many of the game's heroes as characters from the famous Chinese tale *Journey to the West*. The team also themes content like icons around the animal associated with the current year of the lunar calendar.

SPRAYS

JANICE CHU, QIU FANG, AND **AQUATIC MOON**

As with the other seasonal events, Lunar New Year features a unique game mode: Capture the Flag. "At the time when we were coming up with the event, one of the developers was really excited about Capture the Flag, and they mocked up a test of it. We tried it and we thought, 'Yeah. This would be really fun.' So we tied it to the event," said Michael Heiberg. "Afterward, we thought it was broadly appealing, so we shouldn't tie it to just Lunar

New Year. We added it to the normal arcade rotation. When Lunar New Year comes around each time, we just have to try and think of new things to do. It makes it a little more challenging for that event. For example, we added CTF Blitz in 2020, which is a hyper-fast-paced version of the Capture the Flag game mode. We bring the flags together and have much more heated combat."

ICONS

BLACK LILY

▶ **DRAGON SPRAYS** —The team continued the Dragon Dance, its main Lunar New Year spray, by updating it each year for the new heroes. Each hero holds a different part of a long, colorful dragon, which players can connect together in-game.

TOP: **ARNOLD TSANG**; BOTTOM: **AQUATIC MOON**

MAGISTRATE

TOP: **DAVID KANG**; BOTTOM: **AQUATIC MOON**

▶ **CARDINAL BEASTS** —In 2018, the team settled on a unique theme to model many of the icons, sprays, and skins around: mythologies related to four beasts that represent the cardinal directions. The four cardinal beasts of Chinese mythology are tied into astrology and are representative of different elements, directions, and other meanings. "Behind this mythology there is an existing lore—there are all of these relationships. Like the blue dragon is a general of some army in the east, and he has a rivalry with the white tiger of the west. And the phoenix represents reincarnation. In my head, it kind of fits with what was happening with the characters," said concept artist Qiu Fang, who designed the set of skins for 2018. "For these skins, the idea was that Genji got defeated by this blue dragon, which is Pharah, and then he was dying and the witch of the south, who is Mercy, put his soul into a suit of armor. Kind of like how in the Overwatch story Mercy put him back together as a cyborg."

ZHUQUE

QUINGLONG

Apart from just tying elements of Overwatch's lore to the mythology, Fang and the team also incorporated traits of the four beasts into each skin. "Zarya specifically was a turtle and snake together. I was originally trying to have both animals reflected on the armor and weapon somehow," he said. "Eventually I thought it would be cool if we put the turtle theme on the character and put the snake on the weapon, and that worked out."

XUANWU

BAIHU

丫將

▶ **HONG GILDONG TRACER** —Tracer's skin was based off Hong Gildong, a Korean mythological figure and trickster deity who helps the poor and fools the rich. Concept artist Qiu Fang drew inspiration from existing depictions of the character, which featured white pants, a blue vest, a hat, and a scarf around the head. But he also wanted to allude to the fact that this mythological figure rides around on a cloud—a challenge, considering Tracer wouldn't be able to do that in-game.

"I ended up combining the cloud into the character as a pattern and as a motif. It had a little bit more of a theme to it as well. Even if you don't know the character itself, you're like, 'Oh it's a cloud theme,'" said Fang.

GUAN YU

TOP: **QIU FANG**; BOTTOM: **LIPAN LIU**

ZHUGE LIANG

ZHANG FEI

TOP: **LLIA YU**; BOTTOM: **MOXUAN ZHANG**

▶ **THREE KINGDOMS** — In 2019, the team designed skins based on the classic Three Kingdoms story. Nearly all the skins represented famous characters from the tale, such as Reinhardt, who was reimagined as the military commander Guan Yu. In previous years, a single artist might have created the designs. This year, many different individuals created the skins. "They were all done by different Chinese artists," said Tsang. "Some from our internal concept team and others from artists we collaborated with outside of Blizzard."

For Reaper's Lü Bu skin, concept artist Qiu Fang encountered a challenge with the two long tails that extend from his head. That element was critical to representing the Lü Bu character, but the team was concerned that it would negatively impact gameplay.

LÜ BU

HUANG ZHONG

"Generally, we try to avoid that kind of thing because if you're hiding behind cover or something, you'd just expose yourself. There are also clipping issues," said Fang. "Eventually we had to flatten it, and halfway down it becomes a trail of smoke, which is great because it combines Reaper the character with Lü Bu the character."

TOP: **QIU FANG**; BOTTOM: **SHAN QIAO**

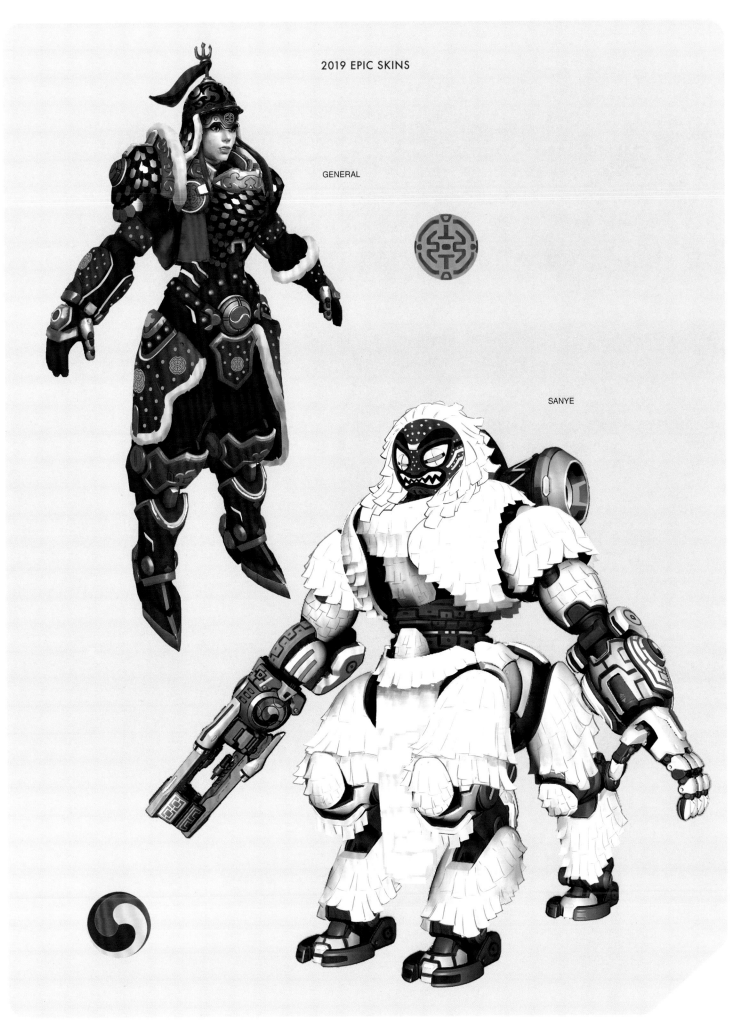

2019 EPIC SKINS

GENERAL

SANYE

ALL IMAGES: **DAVID KANG**

▶ **FACE CHANGER SOMBRA** —For 2020, the developers took a slightly different approach to the content. Rather than creating designs related to a specific story or mythology, the team broadened the theme to encompass aspects of theater and dance from across East Asia.

Sombra was based on ancient Sichuan opera, where masked dancers deftly change their appearance with quick hand gestures. "We worked it into the game so that after a short period of time, Sombra's mask would digitally change," said Tsang. "It fit well into her character because she's a hacker trying to hide her identity."

The team designed the actual masks based on a variety of sources, from themes that appear in Sichuan opera to Sombra's sugar skull icon and skin. "Another was an interpretation of what an omnic Sichuan mask would look like," said Tan, who worked on the skin. "The rest were plays on shapes and colors to create our own mask designs."

SAMUL NORI

TOP: **DARYL TAN**; BOTTOM: **DAVID KANG**

MASK DANCER

OPERA

TOP: **DAVID KANG**; BOTTOM: **DARYL TAN**

▶ **BULL DEMON ORISA** — In 2017, the developers created Lunar New Year skins themed around *Journey to the West*, such as a version of Winston as Sun Wukong, the Monkey King. For 2021, they returned to this influential Chinese story to reimagine Orisa.

"2021 was the Year of the Ox. When I heard I would design skins for Orisa, I knew I was going to do one inspired by the Bull Demon King from *Journey to the West*," said Wang, who worked on the skin. "When I finished my initial ideation sketch, I felt that it was visually too close to the Demon Orisa skin we already had. So I changed the color scheme from warm colors to cooler bluish colors, and I added more scale armor around her body."

Wang looked to armor from the Chinese Han and Tang dynasties for inspiration. He took some of the motifs from those time periods and applied them to Orisa's design. "As for the head, since Orisa is a robotic character, it made sense to turn the bull head into a more hard-surface design so that it would fit with the rest of her body."

▶ **KKACHI ECHO** — Echo's Lunar New Year skin for 2021 drew inspiration from the magpie bird, which symbolizes prosperity and good fortune. "It's good for the beginning of the year," said Kang, who designed the skin. "I think this was the first time we put in so many feathers in one of our heroes, so it is now a staple guideline on what we can do with feathers on other characters in the future."

TOP: **KEJUN WANG**; BOTTOM: **DAVID KANG**

藥

PALE SERPENT

DRAGONFIRE

TOP: **TIM GUO**; BOTTOM: **KEJUN WANG**

TIGER HUNTRESS

ALL IMAGES: **DAVID KANG**

2020 EPIC SKINS

TERRACOTTA MEDIC

IMPERIAL GUARD

XIAKE

ALL IMAGES: **KEJUN WANG**

As developers and as players, the designers had always wanted to expand *Overwatch* beyond a PVP shooter and introduce different, compelling game modes. Their chance came in the form of the Archives events.

"All of the gameplay in the original version of *Overwatch* was against other players. We wanted to create something that had a different tone to it and, at the same time, tell more story in the game," said game director Aaron Keller. "In PVP, the emphasis is on moment-to-moment gameplay, and that means there are fewer story opportunities. With the Archive events, we tried to put as much lore and as much story in them as we could."

A tertiary benefit of the Archives event was that they allowed the team to explore new technologies, art forms, and gameplay mechanics. To create the event's story-driven PVE missions, the developers had to make new AI and spawning systems. They also had to flesh out enemies like Null Sector and Talon.

Everything they learned would help them in the future when they began work on *Overwatch 2*. But first and foremost, their emphasis was on making the Archives events live up to their name.

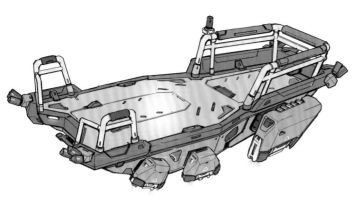

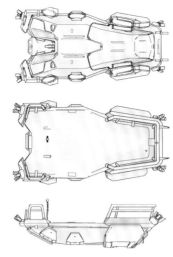

RETRIBUTION

In 2017, the team created the first Archives event: Uprising. The PVE mission revolved around a team of Overwatch agents—Tracer, Torbjörn, Mercy, and Reinhardt—sent into King's Row to stop an attack by Null Sector. It was clear from the community's reaction to Uprising that players were excited about PVE, and they wanted more. For the Retribution event in 2018, the developers created a new story-based mission based around Blackwatch—a covert wing of the Overwatch organization.

"It was an opportunity to see characters in different states than we know them in present-day *Overwatch*," said the game's former lead writer, Michael Chu.

As with Uprising, the team created skins, sprays, icons, and other content alongside the PVE mission. Their guiding principle was to draw on lore for these new pieces of art. When the designers brainstormed what ideas to pursue, they often looked to see if they'd already done an origin skin for a hero. If they hadn't, they seized the opportunity.

For 2018, nearly all of the skins touched on a canonical aspect of the heroes' past: Reyes when he was part of an enhanced soldier program in the United States military, before he became Reaper; Sombra in an outfit showing her allegiance to Talon; and Moira in her Blackwatch uniform, before she left the organization and joined Talon.

TOP: **AL CRUTCHLEY**; BOTTOM: **NESSKAIN**

▶ **BLACKWATCH MOIRA** —Moira's skin was first made public in her origin story. The team had originally wanted to release it as one of her launch skins, but they ultimately decided to save it for the Archives event. Early concepts for the skin, created by Arnold Tsang, featured a white-and-black color scheme that the team felt was too similar to Mercy. When concept artist Qiu Fang stepped in to work on the design, giving Moira a distinct look was just one of the creative challenges he faced.

"Part of the struggle was how to deal with her sleeves, how do we make her head more different, and how do we make it look less like Mercy?" he said.

Moira's long sleeves are an iconic part of her base design, but Fang and the team ultimately removed them from her Blackwatch skin. For her head, the designers gave her a beret, which helped make the hero feel younger than her present-day appearance.

"The third thing was trying to make her look a little different from Mercy. We wanted to keep that overall value breakdown of darker everywhere else with a lighter torso," said Fang. "But having white or a gray just felt too much like Mercy. So my solution there was something a little more evil feeling— the chrome material, which was more unique for her."

SOLDIER: 24

ALL IMAGES: **QIU FANG**

SPECIMEN 28

WINSTON

28

TALON

TOP: **ANH DANG**; BOTTOM LEFT: **QIU FANG**; BOTTOM RIGHT: **MORTEN SKAALVIK**

SCION

TALON

TALON ENEMY CONCEPTS

CHAIN GUN

HEAVY ASSAULT

ENFORCER

TROOPER

ASSASSIN

SNIPER

ALL IMAGES: **QIU FANG**

TALON VEHICLE AND PROP CONCEPTS

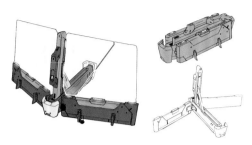

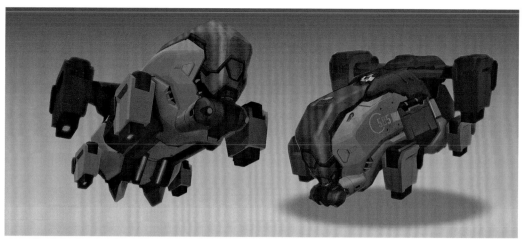

TALON DROPSHIP IDEATION

LEFT: **AL CRUTCHLEY**; RIGHT AND BOTTOM: **QIU FANG**

SPRAYS —Former concept artist Anh Dang created a set of sprays for the Retribution event, based on the enemies that players fight in the PVE mission. "I think in my head I had personalities for the different Talon units, even though in the game they don't have that."

ANH DANG AND ANDREW HOU

IGC —"The Plan" had laid the groundwork for creating in-game cinematics in *Overwatch*, and Retribution took it a step further. The PVE mission revolves around Blackwatch agents Reyes, Moira, Genji, and McCree infiltrating a Talon base to apprehend Antonio, one of Talon's ranking members. But things don't go exactly as planned. Reyes assassinates Antonio, alerting the crime syndicate to Blackwatch's presence and kicking off the mission: a daring escape through the streets of Venice.

For Retribution, director Jason Hill and the team blended the cinematic style and lessons they had learned from "The Plan" and the preceding Archives mission, Uprising. This time around, they included an IGC for the intro and a motion-story for the outro.

DOOR BREACHER ITERATIONS

By using an IGC for the intro, Hill and the team found a way to get players excited about the mission at hand and to create a seamless blend between the cinematic and gameplay. Crafting the outro as a 2.5-D cinematic offered them a different opportunity—a way to create a sense of aftermath to the mission. McCree's voiceover, which accompanies the illustrations, allows the character and viewers to reflect on what happened and the role it played in Overwatch history.

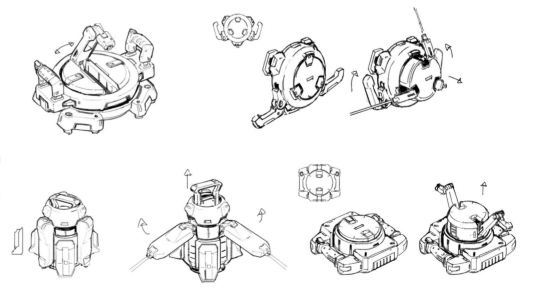

TOP: **LLIA YU**; BOTTOM: **AL CRUTCHLEY**

NESSKAIN

STORM RISING

In 2019, the Archives event took players from the moonlit canals of Venice to the vibrant streets of Havana. Storm Rising told the story of Sojourn, Tracer, Winston, Mercy, and Genji on a mission to apprehend Maximilien, one of Talon's most influential power brokers.

For the PVE mission, the team wove together gameplay, art, and writing so that each element supported the mission's mood and story. Case in point: the dynamic environment the designers created for Storm Rising. As the Overwatch agents pursue Maximilien during the mission, a fierce hurricane barrels toward the city. The approaching storm ratchets up the intensity and creates a sense that time is running out—that Maximilien will slip through Overwatch's fingers if they can't get to him soon.

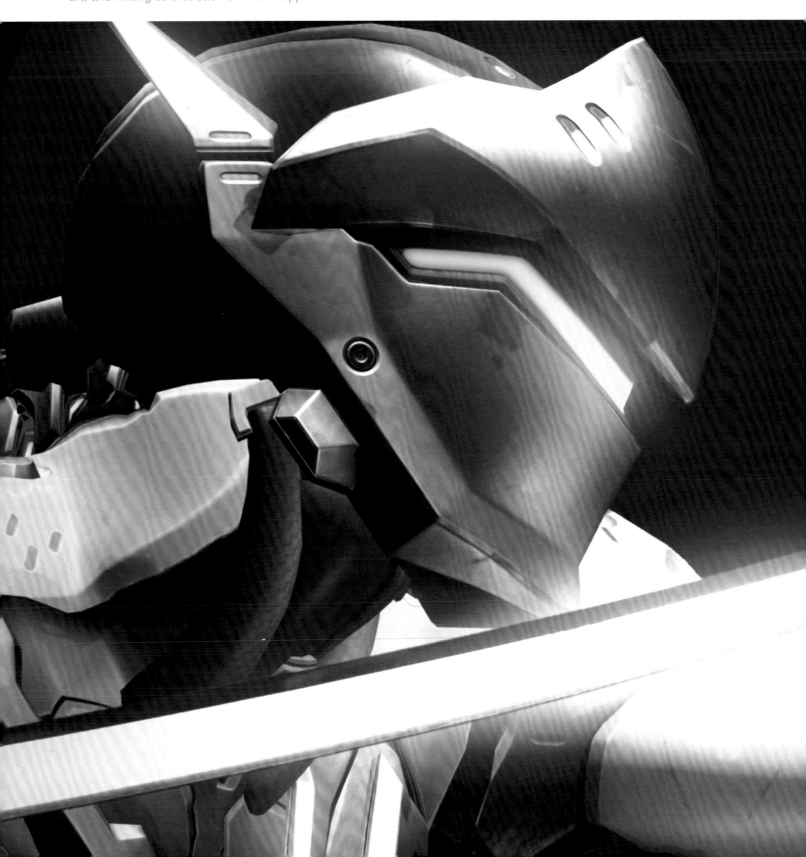

What the team accomplished with Storm Rising was made possible by the work they had done on previous Archives events—and the lessons they had learned in the process. "Retribution was a lot of fun, but it was also pretty fast-paced, and you were always moving. Some amount of the pacing of Uprising was missing. In that one, there were times when you could stop and relax a little bit," said principal game designer Michael Heiberg. "We tried to add a little bit more of that back in Storm Rising. For example, we slowed people down so they can enjoy more of the scenery and the space they're fighting through by putting in a payload."

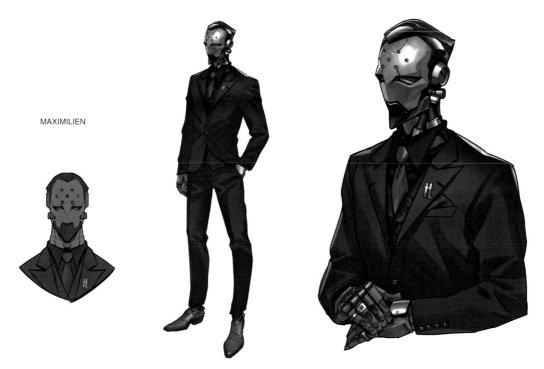

MAXIMILIEN

▶ **IGC** —Storm Rising was the first Archives event to feature IGCs for both the intro and outro. Artists, designers, and filmmakers on the team worked hand in hand to share assets and create a seamless experience between the IGCs and the game. These cinematics were longer and more ambitious than any that had appeared in previous missions.

"I didn't want us to be scared of trying new things," said Jason Hill, who directed the IGCs. "And that's why there's a dynamic energy to Storm Rising. We were thinking, 'Okay, how far do we want to push this thing?'"

As the film begins, Tracer darts into Havana's streets on a hoverbike and chases down Maximilien, a high-ranking member of the Talon organization. Artists and designers collaborated on the design of Tracer's vehicle to make sure it captured the right

feel and level of technology. They explored several concepts, some of which drew inspiration from Tracer's test pilot background. Others looked more like a vehicle belonging to the Overwatch organization.

"We settled on an Overwatch mission bike, rather than just Tracer's personal bike," said senior environment artist Al Crutchley. "We incorporated the color distribution and values of existing Overwatch tech to make the vehicle."

The high-speed, action-packed chase also presented an enormous challenge for the team. The in-game map was smaller than what the designers required for the scene, and they built a custom set to accommodate it. This allowed the filmmakers to extend the street by copying different sets of buildings, thereby creating a larger area to stage the thrilling chase.

▶ **EQUALIZER LÚCIO** —Lúcio's Equalizer skin was rooted both in lore and in one of the hero's original concepts. A DJ skin already seemed a perfect fit for Lúcio's backstory as a freedom-fighting DJ, and after concept art of the skin was featured in *The Art of Overwatch, Volume 1*, members of the community started asking for it to be introduced into the game. The team delivered with Equalizer, which drew on retro elements like a Walkman and roller skates, and also contained equalizing bars that jump in real time.

TOP RIGHT: **MORTEN SKAALVIK**; BOTTOM: **ARNOLD TSANG**

▶ **PAJAMEI MEI** — Mei's skin was based on her design from the "Rise and Shine" cinematic. In the story, she builds her ice gun out of parts she finds around the Ecopoint, such as a blow dryer. The issue the team ran into was they had already used that idea for Mei's Ecopoint: Antarctica skin. "We didn't want to do it again, so we went with her Pajama outfit and aligned her Endothermic Blaster more with the morning theme: tea," said Tsang. "She's making it at the beginning of the short. The mug is from the cinematic as well. The two dogs on it are actually cinematic director Ben Dai's dogs."

SUMMER GAMES

The skins created for Storm Rising continued the theme from previous Archives events, depicting heroes how they looked in the past. Artists created a Talon skin for Baptiste, based on his previous tenure with the organization. The Formal: 76 skin was inspired by an illustration of Jack Morrison receiving a medal in *Overwatch*'s original announcement trailer. "Deadlock McCree was from his time in the Deadlock Gang," said Tsang. "He's supposed to be seventeen, before he lost his arm."

One exception to these canonical skins was Gwishin Bastion, which was more of a reimagining of the hero. "We tied it to the lore about Gwishin omnics from the 'Shooting Star' D.Va animated short," said Tsang. "What if Bastion was from that family of omnics?"

FORMAL: 76

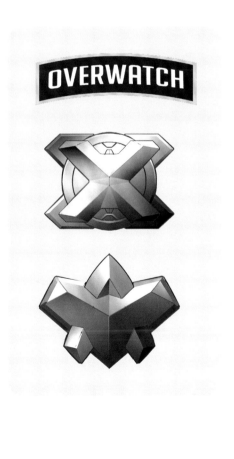

▶ **SOCIALITE ASHE** —Socialite Ashe drew from the hero's wealthy and exuberant upbringing. "Ashe is the leader of the Deadlock Gang, but she's also a rich girl. She grew up very fancy, and so we leaned into that for this," said former concept artist Anh Dang, who designed the skin alongside Ben Zhang and Morten Skaalvik. "Her dynamite has the quilted patterns that you see on purses. Even the gun itself is Art Deco."

TOP: **ANH DANG**; BOTTOM: **BEN ZHANG** AND **MORTEN SKAALVIK**

DEADLOCK

TALON

TOP: **BEN ZHANG**; BOTTOM LEFT: **QIU FANG**; BOTTOM RIGHT: **DARYL TAN**

GWISHIN

SCIENTIST

TOP: **MORTEN SKAALVIK**; BOTTOM RIGHT: **ARNOLD TSANG** AND **QIU FANG**

2020

For 2020, the team did not create a new PVE mission, but they did continue crafting skins, sprays, and icons inspired by who the heroes are and where they came from. Some of the designs took a different approach from previous years, drawing more on cultural and thematic aspects of the characters. For example, Symmetra's skin was made to coincide with the Holi festival, which was held around the time of the Archives event. Pharah's Aviator skin was a celebration of fan art that had existed, depicting the hero as a hotshot pilot in aviator glasses and leather jacket. She also appeared in the outfit in the second issue of the *New Blood* comic.

▶ **KING JAMISON JUNKRAT** —Junkrat's skin wasn't entirely canonical, but it did tie into the backstory of the hero pilfering valuables from across the world. The designers layered in references from a variety of sources: the famous Crown Jewels of England, a monkey artifact from *Hearthstone*'s League of Explorers expansion, and a sword and shield based on the awards that Blizzard Entertainment gives to employees who reach five and ten years of service.

MILITIA

ALL IMAGES: **DAVID KANG**

▶ **WORKOUT ZARYA** —Zarya's skin was the brainchild of former concept artist Anh Dang. She created the design based on her own love of weightlifting as well as the hero's backstory as an international weightlifting champion. "During this time, I got really into weightlifting, so this skin is just all the stuff I like. It was very special." Based on her athletic experience, Dang incorporated little details into the skin like the type of clothing and monitor worn by Zarya.

AVIATOR

TOP: **ANH DANG**; BOTTOM: **DAVID KANG**

▶ **SNIPER ANA** —For Ana's skin, the team drew inspiration from the time she spent in the Egyptian military as an elite sniper. The trick was finding the right kind of outfit—something that would be visually interesting but also preserve her silhouette. Concept artist Daryl Tan created a ghillie suit that would mimic the general shape of her base coat.

"Her gun has a more modern military look to it," said Tan. "We make interesting geometric shapes that are different from the base skin, but we have to take into consideration the hard points. There are a lot of areas where specific animation is needed. Like how a magazine goes in, where an empty casing ejects from, where the scope is. With Ana, she had a pretty small scope on her base gun, so we couldn't push the size of the scope to be huge like the ones on modern sniper rifles."

ALL IMAGES: **DARYL TAN**

2020 EPIC SKINS

BUBBLE GUM

HOLI

TOXIC

For 2021, the team decided to do something completely different with its approach to skins. Instead of designing the heroes to represent periods from their *own* past, they imagined the characters in historical uniforms worn by soldiers from their countries of origin. Cavalry Tracer was a design that the team had wanted to do long before this Archives event, and it was based on some of the hero's first skin concepts.

The designers didn't move forward with the Cavalry skin at the time, but they revisited it for this event. The team brought on Japanese artist Yusuke Kozaki to create his own take on the idea, as well as a skin of Soldier: 76 as an American Revolutionary War soldier.

CAVALRY

POLYANITSA

TOP: **YUSUKE KOZAKI**; BOTTOM: **YIMING LIU**

MOUSQUETAIRE

SOLDIER: 1776

TOP: **MORTEN SKAALVIK**; BOTTOM: **YUSUKE KOZAKI**; BOTTOM RIGHT: **DARYL TAN**

BUSHI

CAMOUFLAGE

SUBAQUATIC

TOP: **ARMANDO GONZALEZ-DORTA**; BOTTOM: **DARYL TAN**

ANNIVERSARY

Anniversary is held on May 24, the day of *Overwatch*'s release, but it was never intended to be a self-congratulatory event. "We want to celebrate the community," said Michael Heiberg. "We want to celebrate the players who are actually making this a game."

The designers also saw the Anniversary event as a place for artists to let their imaginations run wild. "We had done Summer Games, Halloween Terror, Winter Wonderland, Archives, Lunar New Year—and we had forced the art team to stick to very strict themes for each," said *Overwatch*'s former game director, Jeff Kaplan. "I remember the artists kind of thinking, 'We have all these great ideas, they just don't fit into anything we're doing.' And so Anniversary actually came more from a desire to free the artists to explore any cool idea that they wanted."

Artists were encouraged to stretch their wings and chase their passions. Some of the skins created for Anniversary tied into aspects of the lore, such as Doomfist's formal outfit, which was inspired by his appearance in the *Masquerade* comic and the outro cinematic for Storm Rising. Other skins, like Bilgerat Junkrat, were simply created because they seemed like fun concepts that were rich with potential for compelling visual designs.

STEALTH

FOREST SPIRIT

TOP: **QIU FANG**; BOTTOM: **BEN ZHANG**

MAGICIAN

FORMAL

TOP LEFT: **MATTEO DE LONGIS**; TOP RIGHT: **ANH DANG**; BOTTOM: **QIU FANG**

2018

SHIELD MAIDEN

BILGERAT

TOP: **MORTEN SKAALVIK**; BOTTOM: **LIPAN LIU**

SHERLOCK

CYBJÖRN

[⚠ CAUTION]

▶ **ACADEMY D.VA** —For D.Va's Academy skin, the team leaned into aspects of her backstory. They based the mech design off the game she played in high school: *Mecha Guardian V.* While she was still a student, she won the world championship for the game and became famous in the pro gaming world. Hints about D.Va's past were also incorporated into the Busan map. "If you're in Busan MEKA Base and look at the rooms for the pilots, on the PC you can see the menu screen for that game," said Tsang.

HONEYDEW

TOP AND BOTTOM LEFT: **DAVID KANG**; BOTTOM RIGHT: **QIU FANG**

▶ **GARGOYLE WINSTON** —Winston's new skin incorporated elements from gargoyles and medieval Gothic churches. The red glow bleeding through the cracks on his stone skin hints at the power and fury that lies within. "I thought it was pretty cool that it matched Winston—gargoyles break out of their mold and come alive," said concept artist David Kang, who designed the skin. "And that's kind of what Winston does when he's using his ultimate ability. He becomes entirely red."

ORBITAL

ALL IMAGES: **DAVID KANG**

TOXIC

▶ **HUITZILOPOCHTLI**—Zenyatta is a deeply spiritual and empathetic omnic monk. He has traveled the world to learn from other cultures, seek knowledge, and forge meaningful connections with the people he meets. The team crafted this skin to show how the hero learns from different religions, mythologies, and ways of life.

TOP: **ARNOLD TSANG**; BOTTOM: **MORTEN SKAALVIK**

2020

LITTLE RED

ALL IMAGES: **QIU FANG** AND **KEJUN WANG**

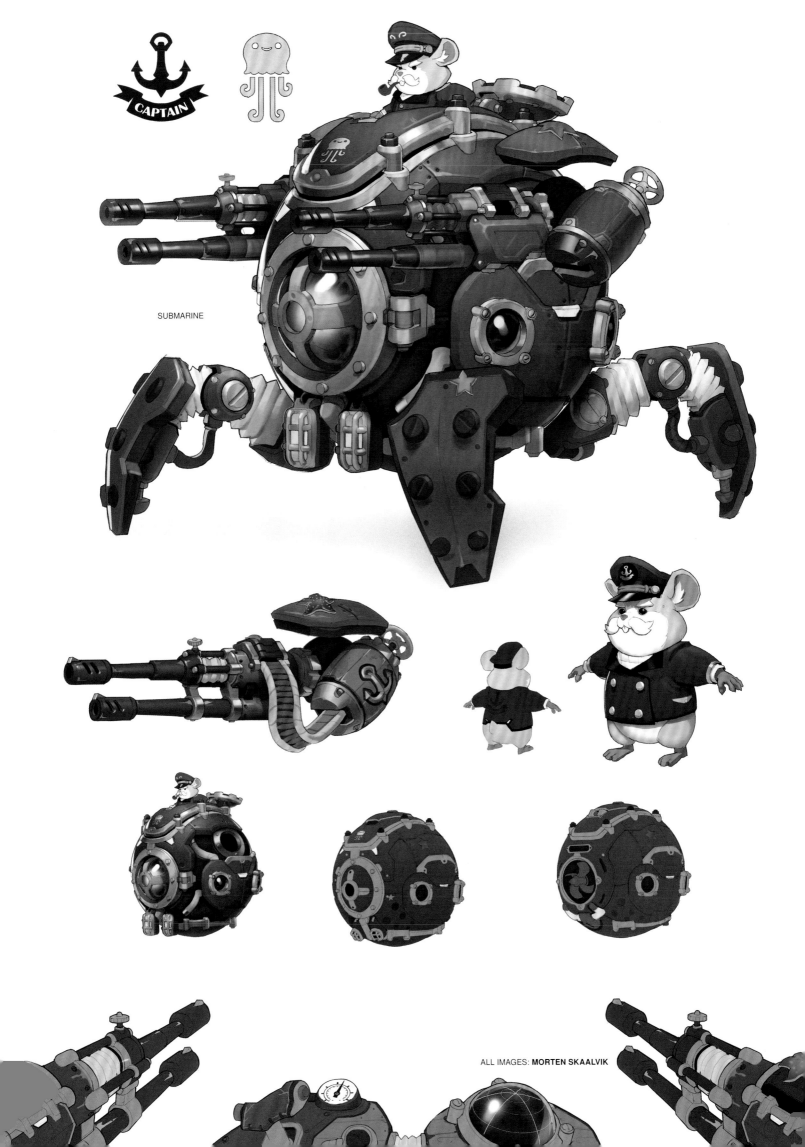

CAPTAIN

SUBMARINE

ALL IMAGES: **MORTEN SKAALVIK**

DRAGOON

MASQUERADE

TOP: **DAVID KANG**; BOTTOM: **ANH DANG**

Groovy

FUNKY

BLACK CAT

JUNKFOOD

GLADIATOR

TOP: **DAVID KANG**; BOTTOM: **ARNOLD TSANG** AND **ANH DANG**

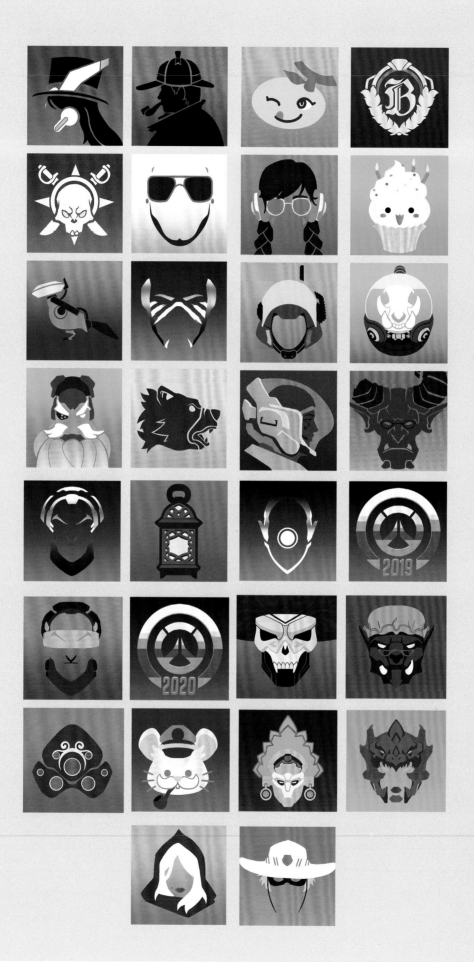

ALL IMAGES: **AQUATIC MOON, ANDREW HOU,** AND **QIU FANG**

NESSKAIN

CHALLENGES

Apart from main events like Lunar New Year and Archives, the team found other opportunities to release content. D.Va's Nano Cola Challenge was the first of these "mini-events," and it set the stage for many others that would follow.

CHALLENGES

D.VA'S NANO COLA CHALLENGE

"D.Va's Nano Cola Challenge was an experiment. We were brainstorming different ways to engage players," said Tsang. "It was around the time we made 'Shooting Star,' and we had an idea for a Nano Cola D.Va skin that appeared on posters in the cinematic."

The team created this skin of D.Va, originally concepted by visual development artist Jungah Lee, and released it along with a number of similarly themed sprays and player icons. "We didn't plan for it to be an ongoing thing—it was just something we tried," said Tsang. "But we got a positive response, so we kept doing it."

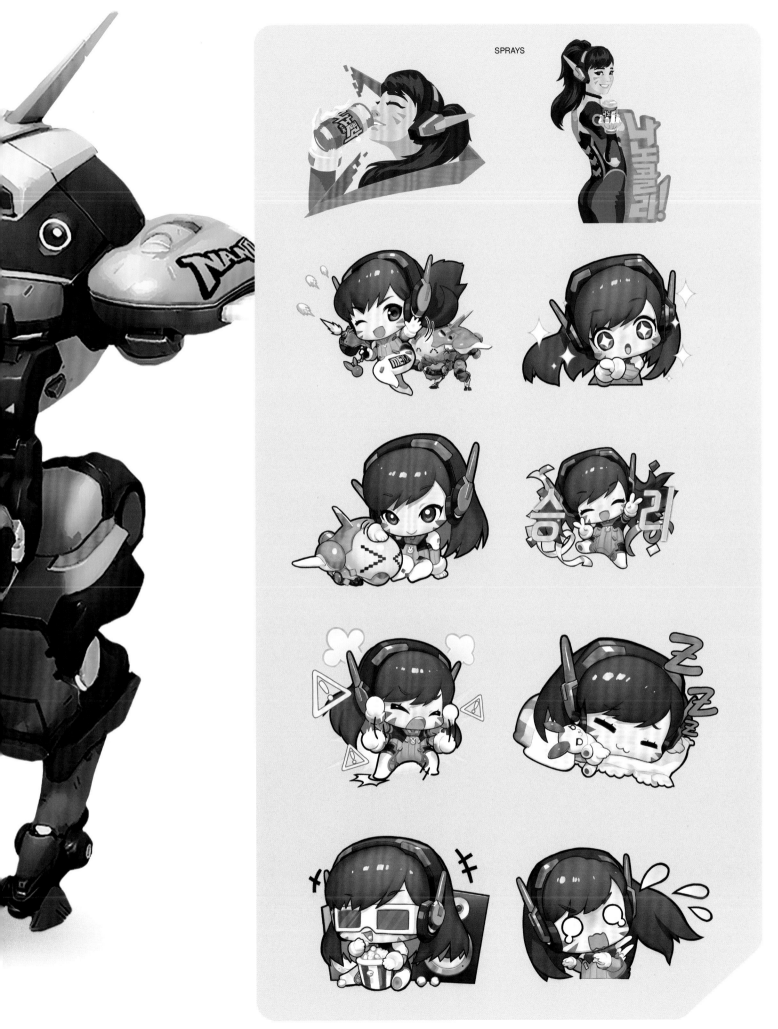

SPRAYS

ANA'S BASTET CHALLENGE

ANA'S BASTET CHALLENGE

After Nano Cola, the designers were eager to do a similar mini-event, but they wanted it to have a meaningful connection to the game. "We felt like what made Nano Cola successful was because it was anchored to the 'Shooting Star' animated short," said Tsang. "For the next event, we approached it from skin design first. We designed the Bastet skin for Ana, which inspired the story for the event."

What they created to accompany the skin was "Bastet," *Overwatch*'s first short story. Written by former lead writer Michael Chu and featuring illustrations by Tsang, the tale revealed new details about Ana, a former leader of the Overwatch organization who had gone into hiding.

ALL IMAGES: **ARNOLD TSANG**

"BASTET" SHORT STORY ILLUSTRATIONS

BAPTISTE'S REUNION CHALLENGE

The mini-events were a constant learning experience for the team; each one gave them a better idea of what was working. After the "Bastet" short story, the designers were pleased to find that players enjoyed learning about the story of *Overwatch* and its heroes, and so the team aimed to deliver more. The next mini-event revolved around another short story, "What You Left Behind."

"We were developing this idea right around when Baptiste launched," said Tsang. "He didn't have too many close relationships with existing heroes."

Written by Alyssa Wong and illustrated by Tsang, "What You Left Behind" explores more of Baptiste's origins and anchors him firmly in the Overwatch universe. One of the side characters featured in the story is Mauga, who was originally planned to be a new hero before the team replaced him with Sigma. But the team liked the Mauga character so much, they wanted to tie him into Baptiste's lore.

ALL IMAGES: **ARNOLD TSANG**

"WHAT YOU LEFT BEHIND" SHORT STORY ILLUSTRATIONS

SPRAYS

BASTION'S BRICK CHALLENGE

When *Overwatch*'s designers partnered with the legendary toymaker The LEGO Group, they were already imagining a skin for Bastion. But rather than simply release the skin on its own, they crafted a mini-event to shine a light on the partnership. "This was a big deal for us," said Tsang. "The concept was very fun to work on, but also very hard."

ICONS

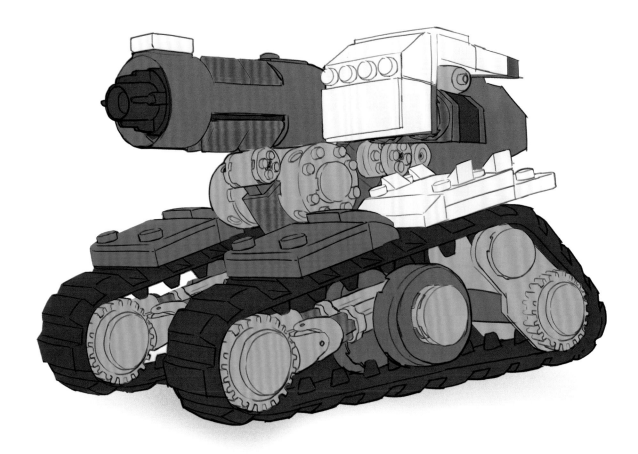

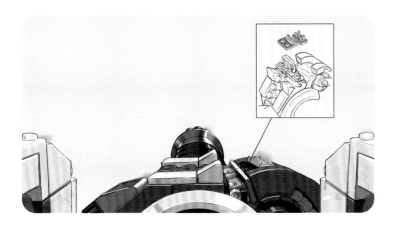

The LEGO Group has rules about how its pieces are represented in other mediums. For example, the studs where pieces connect must have a consistent scale across the entire model. "We had the actual Bastion LEGO set to reference, but because of the way those are built, they had to make decisions that changed the hero's proportions," said Tsang. "The limitation for us was having to match Bastion's proportions one-to-one with the game model. We had to scale some pieces slightly, but it had to appear to be built with actual LEGO bricks. It was a fun challenge to tackle."

ALL IMAGES: **ARNOLD TSANG** AND **DARYL TAN**

MERCY'S RECALL CHALLENGE

MERCY'S RECALL CHALLENGE

Mercy is one of *Overwatch*'s most popular heroes, but before "Valkyrie" was created, her backstory had not been fleshed out in much detail. The short story, written by Michael Chu, explored the character's past and current whereabouts, and the mini-event crafted around it offered a new skin and an array of content for players.

SPRAYS

LEFT: **VICKI TSAI**; TOP RIGHT: **ARNOLD TSANG**; BOTTOM RIGHT: **NESSKAIN**

"VALKYRIE" SHORT STORY ILLUSTRATIONS

Some of the sprays were based on the short story's illustrations, which were created by Nesskain. This was the first time the artist, who had worked on a number of *Overwatch*'s origin motion stories, made content for a short story.

CHALLENGES

ASHE'S MARDI GRAS CHALLENGE

Much like Nano Cola, the Mardi Gras event came about as something of a chance opportunity. "We had a little window for live content, and we wanted to fill it with something," said Tsang. "For this specific time slot on the calendar, it was around Mardi Gras. So we thought it would be a fun one to celebrate."

The Ashe skin is more representative of how the United States celebrates Mardi Gras, but the team made sprays to explore how the holiday is celebrated in other countries.

SPRAYS

BOTTOM: **ANDREW HOU**; TOP: **ARNOLD TSANG**

CHALLENGES
SIGMA'S MAESTRO CHALLENGE

The Sigma Maestro event was born from a convergence of different ideas. The team had been working on an *Overwatch* album—Cities and Countries—and they wanted to create a mini-event to bring it to the community's attention. Because of Sigma's affinity for classical music, the designers realized he would be the perfect candidate to feature.

Concept artist Kejun Wang's design for the skin was inspired by the brass instruments featured in the Jazzy Lúcio skin. Using that as a starting point, he focused more on string instruments and modeled Sigma's armor on the shapes of violins.

"In the beginning, I remember his hair was pretty formal and clean cut. I sent out the first ideation, and people said it was too sleek," said Wang. "He has this Einstein-slash-Beethoven vibe. So I messed up his hair to bring this feeling to him."

Animators had separately been working on a new emote for Sigma, portraying him as a conductor. "They realized it would be perfect for this event," said Tsang. "It was the first time we would have an emote as part of the reward structure for a mini-event."

SPRAYS

TOP: **KEJUN WANG**; BOTTOM: **ANDREW HOU**

CHALLENGES

TRACER'S COMIC CHALLENGE

To celebrate the release of the first issue from the five-part *Tracer—London Calling* comic series, the team launched a new mini-event. Tracer's Comic Challenge featured an array of content, including sprays inspired by sound effects from comics. Creating these designs was a huge undertaking from a localization standpoint—the text had to be translated into every language that the game supports.

SPRAY

ARNOLD TSANG AND BABS TARR

For the skin, the team worked with the comic's artist, Babs Tarr, to create a new and compelling Tracer design. "At first we were thinking it's an outfit from the comic, but that wasn't different enough from her base outfit, and she already has a punk skin," said Tsang. "So we had the idea of having comic panels on her leggings. From there this design sprang to life. What was really fun about this was that we collaborated with Babs Tarr. She put her own spin on it when we showed her the early concept."

CENTER: **BENGAL**

SYMMETRA'S RESTORATION CHALLENGE

Like Mercy, Symmetra and Zenyatta were heroes that the designers felt needed a short story to flesh out more of their lore. They turned to senior writer Christie Golden and artist Nesskain to create "Stone by Stone." Building off previous short story releases, the team created a Symmetra skin, icon, and other content for the mini-event. The developers also wanted an artist who had a connection to the story and the main character, Symmetra, to lend their vision to the project. They contracted JaviDraws, based in India, to craft some of the sprays in her own unique style.

TOP LEFT: **JAVERIA KHOSO**; TOP RIGHT: **ARNOLD TSANG**; BOTTOM: **NESSKAIN**

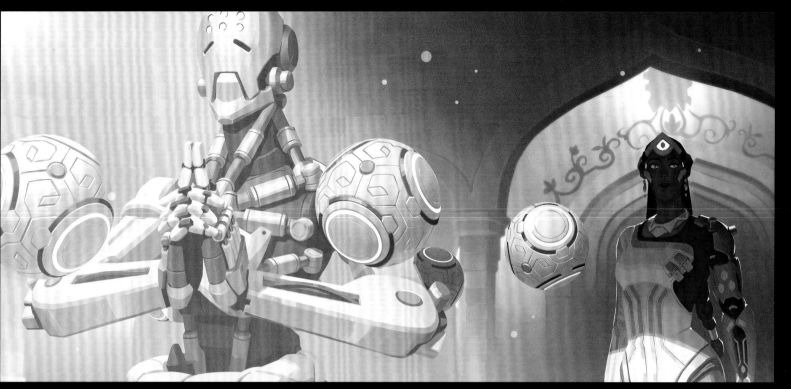

"STONE BY STONE" SHORT STORY ILLUSTRATIONS

SPRAYS

TOP: **NESSKAIN**; LEFT: **JAVERIA KHOSO**

CHALLENGES
KANEZAKA CHALLENGE

The Kanezaka Challenge was the first mini-event centered around a new map release. To build excitement for this new location, the designers created the Kyōgisha Hanzo skin as well as a unique icon and sprays, all of which players could earn as rewards during the event.

Although the Kanezaka Challenge featured a skin, the focus of its rewards was on the location itself. The icon and the sprays all featured elements that players could find on the map. "Usually we want to have character-based sprays, but the good part about the map was we made a lot of signs that have characters as their mascots. The pottery school has a little dog. The mascot for Pugtato—the bag shop—is loosely based on the dog of one of our producers who helps make the maps."

SPRAYS

ALL IMAGES: **KEJUN WANG**

PACHI MARCHI CHALLENGE

CHALLENGES

PACHIMARCHI CHALLENGE

Every March starting in 2019, the Overwatch and Consumer Products teams have worked together to feature pachimari-related products on Blizzard's official gear store. In 2021, they took things a step further and crafted an event to highlight this special time of year: the PachiMarchi Challenge.

Designers created a unique skin for Roadhog showing his love for the cute onion-shaped pachimaris. This aspect of the character was earlier hinted at in the "A Moment in Crime Special Report: 'The Junkers'" origin story, which showed Roadhog storming out of a Japanese arcade with an armful of stolen pachimari plushies.

SPRAYS

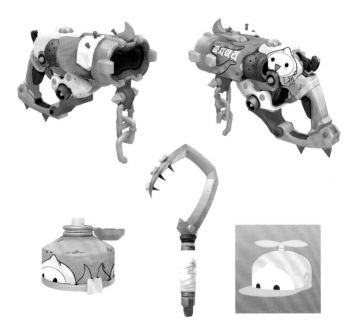

TOP & RIGHT: **DAVID KANG**; BOTTOM LEFT: **MEITINGUAN**

CHALLENGES

ASHE'S DEADLOCK CHALLENGE

As the Overwatch team continued to expand their universe with short stories, long-form fiction came into focus as an exciting new opportunity. After the successful release of *The Hero of Numbani*, which chronicled Orisa's beginnings, the team identified Ashe and McCree's origins with the Deadlock gang as a story ripe for the telling.

The *Deadlock Rebels* young adult novel was published by Scholastic in June 2021 and celebrated with an in-game challenge. Cover artist Xiao Tong Kong had already worked closely with Tsang in crafting Ashe and B.O.B.'s unique cover looks, so it seemed a natural fit to translate those into a new skin. The accompanying sprays—inspired by events in the novel—completed the challenge.

ALL IMAGES: **ARMANDO GONZALEZ-DORTA**

SPRAYS

TOP: **XIAO TONG KONG**; BOTTOM: **ANDREW HOU**

SKINS

Outside of seasonal events, challenges, and launching new heroes, the developers have found many other opportunities to release skins. Charities, BlizzCon, and Overwatch League all offer the chance to explore unique designs.

But how the team approaches creating skins remains consistent across everything. "Like all our other skins, the important thing is you need to keep the general silhouette the same, but you also need to play around to make it look different," said concept artist David Kang.

This balance between creating a fresh take on a character but also preserving the elements of what makes them recognizable is always at the forefront of the designers' minds. Many of the skins created for Overwatch League and BlizzCon combined the heroes with characters from Blizzard's other games as well as real-life esports players and teams. This made for compelling designs, but it also meant that the team had to ensure that the essence of *Overwatch*'s heroes did not get lost.

OVERWATCH LEAGUE™

SKINS

OVERWATCH LEAGUE

The launch of Overwatch League was a momentous occasion for the developers. The game was poised to take a huge step into the world of professional esports, and the team worked tirelessly to blend *Overwatch*'s stylized look with this new venture.

"We were defining the brand of the league. We wanted it to feel like it was part of *Overwatch*—a bright and aspirational future. But we also wanted it to feel like a pro sports league," said *Overwatch*'s former game director, Jeff Kaplan. "We wanted to help the teams pick an identity for themselves that celebrates their location, celebrates *Overwatch*, and also works as a cohesive set for the rest of the league."

A

ATLANTIC

PACIFIC

P

ALL IMAGES: **BEN ZHANG**, **QIU FANG**, **DAVID KANG**, AND **MORTEN SKAALVIK**

ATLANTIC

PACIFIC

Beyond guiding the general look for the league and helping individual teams design their logos and color schemes, the developers created special skins to celebrate the competitive nature of this new esports venture. "We wanted to hype up the community," said former concept artist Ben Zhang. "The *Overwatch* All-Star skins were made for that purpose. Because of the nature of the league, being an esport, we want to have an opposing force idea built into these skins. For the first one we came up with water versus fire. The second year is a day versus night theme."

For each of these sets, the team created customized effects that set them apart from other skins. But that also made the designs extremely challenging to create in-game. "For example, Lúcio's hair is made of fine, thin pieces of cloth. In order to get that floating motion for the hair, I sat down with our rigging team, trying to figure out what is the best way to achieve that kind of motion," said Zhang. "The character, especially for Lúcio, when he's skating around, we wanted to have his hair being pulled by the wind and go along with his momentum. That took a lot of iterations."

2020

CELESTIAL

GAIA

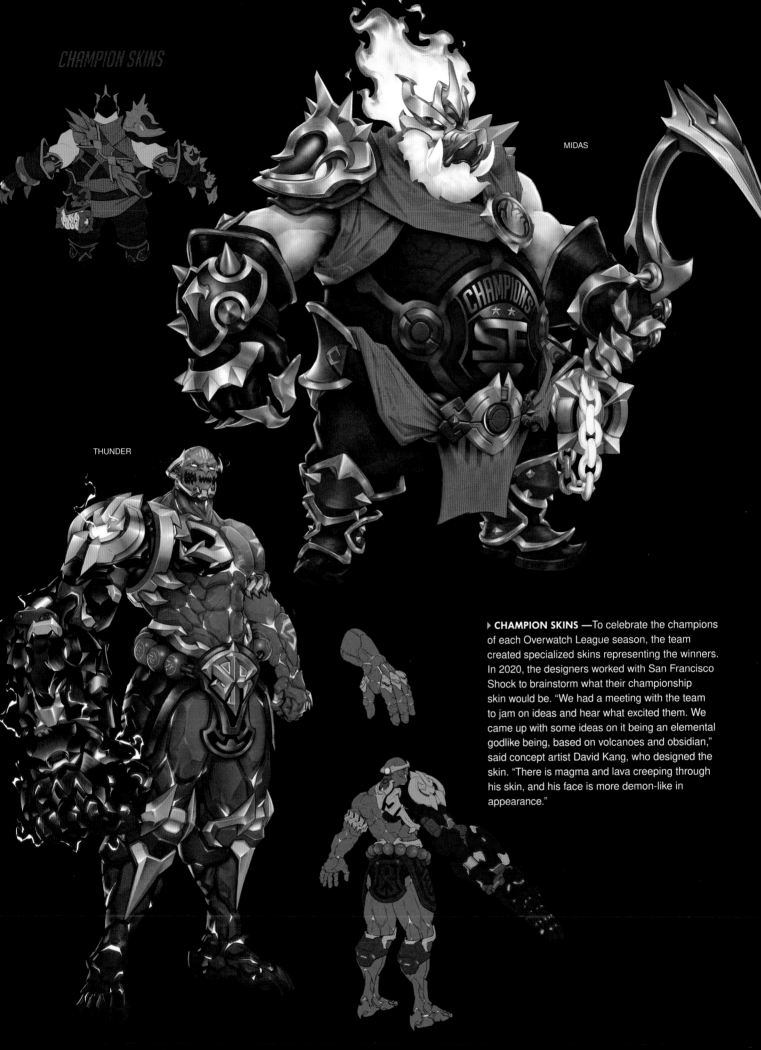

MIDAS

THUNDER

▶ **CHAMPION SKINS** —To celebrate the champions of each Overwatch League season, the team created specialized skins representing the winners. In 2020, the designers worked with San Francisco Shock to brainstorm what their championship skin would be. "We had a meeting with the team to jam on ideas and hear what excited them. We came up with some ideas on it being an elemental godlike being, based on volcanoes and obsidian," said concept artist David Kang, who designed the skin. "There is magma and lava creeping through his skin, and his face is more demon-like in appearance."

ALL IMAGES: **DAVID KANG**

FLYING ACE

MVP SKINS

▶ **MVP SKINS** —The Zen-Nakji skin was created in honor of JJoNak, the professional Overwatch League player on New York Excelsior, and it incorporates a number of different things about him. "His main character is Zenyatta," said Kang, who created the concept. "In some interview he mentioned his favorite animal is an octopus. Along with his team color, we got all these details captured in the skin."

ZEN-NAKJI

GOOD VS. EVIL

GOAT

HAROERIS

TOP: **MORTEN SKAALVIK**; BOTTOM: **QIU FANG**

MM-MEI

ANGE DE LA MORT

TOP: **KEJUN WANG**; BOTTOM: **DAVID KANG**

DEMON
HUNTER

BLIZZCON

Ever since the developers started making *Overwatch*, they had wanted to create skins based on Blizzard's other games. "The way we develop heroes, we try to use archetypes that people are familiar with," said character art director Arnold Tsang. "So it's only natural that Blizzard characters from other universes work well as skins in *Overwatch*. We've always had a list of cool matchups."

The issue was always finding the right time and place to release these skins. They wouldn't have fit with the themes of events like Lunar New Year or Summer Games, but they were the perfect content to release for BlizzCon—a convention that celebrates *all* the company's games.

ALL IMAGES: **BEN ZHANG**

ILLIDAN

TYRANDE

▶ **RAYNHARDT** —The team reimagined Reinhardt as *StarCraft*'s Jim Raynor for BlizzConline, a virtual version of the BlizzCon convention held in 2021. The bulky *Overwatch* hero's proportions matched well with Raynor in his marine armor. The designers found ways to include the character's rounded helmet and shoulder pads, which gave Reinhardt's skin a unique look while also preserving the shape and silhouette of his in-game model.

"Especially after the Blizzard World map came out, we wanted to celebrate Blizzard as a whole," said Tsang. "We felt like it was time, so we started doing the BlizzCon skins as crossover themes."

In 2019, former concept artist Ben Zhang and concept artist Morten Skaalvik created designs based on two of the most revered characters in the Warcraft universe: an Illidan skin for Genji and a Tyrande skin for Symmetra. Throughout the years, the appearance of these characters had gradually evolved, and part of the challenge facing

the team was finding what "era" of these iconic heroes to capture.

"Illidan has a certain look in *Warcraft III*, then a slightly different look in *World of Warcraft*," said Tsang. "The *Warcraft III* form, where he's more night elf, works for us because the proportions are more humanoid. But because that's not as iconic as the *World of Warcraft* look, we tried to land somewhere in the middle. He doesn't have the wings, and the horns aren't gigantic, but it still feels like it's Illidan."

ALL IMAGES: **KEJUN WANG**

LOOTBOX REFRESH

Loot Box Refresh gave the team another opportunity to inject new skins into the game that weren't limited by specific seasonal themes. Like the content released for BlizzCon, many of these designs were crossovers between *Overwatch* heroes and characters from Blizzard's other games.

BLACK CAT

KABUKI

TOP: **LLIA YU**; BOTTOM: **JUNGAH LEE**

ECOPOINT: ANTARCTICA

BARBARIAN

TOP: **JUNGAH LEE**; BOTTOM: **BEN ZHANG**

MAGNI
BRONZEBEARD

BUTCHER

TOP: **MORTEN SKAALVIK**; BOTTOM: **BEN ZHANG**

CAPOEIRA

▶ **BLACKHAND DOOMFIST** —For Doomfist, the team had discussed a Warcraft-themed skin—Blackhand—early on, but releasing it didn't make much sense until after the Blizzard World map was created. "After the map came out, the community loved it," said Zhang, who designed the skin. "So we thought it was the right time to introduce that skin."

Zhang and the other designers took a thoughtful approach to creating this skin, along with all others that involved merging characters from Blizzard's different universes. "When approaching crossovers, it's not just porting them into *Overwatch*," said Zhang. "The first thing we looked for was a likeness between the characters. Blackhand felt like the perfect fit due to the visual similarities with Doomfist."

And like all skins, many of them evolved during the design process. The developers had originally considered making a skin for Torbjörn based off the Warcraft dwarf warrior Muradin, but they were concerned it might feel too much like a viking—a skin that Torbjörn already had. Instead, they made the skin based off another dwarf: Magni.

TOP: **MORTEN SKAALVIK**; BOTTOM: **ANH DANG** AND **BEN ZHANG**

CRUSADER

IMMORTAL

KERRIGAN

NOVA

ICONS

▶ **PINK MERCY** —Unlike other mini-events, it was created to raise money for the Breast Cancer Research Foundation. "It was a huge event for us, and we wanted to do something for charity," said Tsang. "For the skin itself, we wanted to theme it around breast cancer research and awareness. Mercy made sense because she's a doctor and a woman—she's also a very popular character. We wanted to put our best foot forward for this cause."

As Tsang designed the skin, former concept artist Anh Dang concepted Mercy's weapon, drawing inspiration from shōjo anime. "It definitely has a magical girl feel. She's got her pigtails, her big magic wand staff. Everything is pink and covered in ribbons," said Dang. "I draw a lot of sci-fi and mechs, but I have a soft spot for pink weapons I guess."

Beyond just visual art, the team added an audio detail to make the skin unique. When Mercy fully heals someone in-game, a bell rings.

SPRAYS

BOTTOM LEFT: **ONEMEGAWATT**; TOP: **ARNOLD TSANG**; BOTTOM RIGHT: **ANH DANG**

ANIMATED SHORTS

Animated shorts have been a part of *Overwatch* since the game was first announced at BlizzCon in 2014. An action-packed and heartfelt cinematic featuring Tracer, Winston, Widowmaker, and Reaper revealed this new universe and its heroes to the world. Around the time of the game's release in 2016, the team premiered a handful of other animated shorts, each one revolving around a different character.

In 2017, the team developed another wave of animated shorts. Some of these cinematics teased upcoming heroes and were staged in locations that were being simultaneously developed for the game. To maintain consistency between the two mediums, the creators fostered a culture of collaboration. They shared assets, ideas, and learned lessons, which helped the team create a unified style between the cinematics and the game.

While the goal of creating compelling stories was still the same, the developers also made a conscious decision to carry on an overarching narrative established in the preceding cinematics—that of Winston sending out a recall to the former members of Overwatch. "We knew we needed something to tie it all together. We had laid some ground in the original," said character art director Arnold Tsang. "With 'Recall,' with Genji getting in touch with Hanzo in 'Dragons'—the vibe is we're getting the group back together. That was the overarching thread we tried to weave into the shorts, but we still focused in on character as well."

"RISE AND SHINE"

Released on August 23, 2017, "Rise and Shine" tells the story of Mei, a kindhearted scientist pushed to face her fears and become a hero. After going into cryogenic hibernation to escape a brutal snowstorm, she awakens to find her life in ruins: years have passed, her remote Antarctica research base is barely functional, and her fellow researchers are dead. With the help of a small robot named Snowball, Mei finds the courage to escape the base and venture back out into the world.

The story is staged in the Ecopoint: Antarctica base, a difficult location because of how much ice and snow is present in the environment. Creating these elements in a stylized world like *Overwatch* is a challenge because

artists and animators run the risk of creating ice that looks too simple or untextured. The team went through many iterations to find the right balance of color and lighting to get the ice right.

Beyond ice and snow, the Antarctica environment influenced the overall color scheme for the animated short. "Blue is a common color in pretty much all the shots, so it plays a huge role," said director Ben Dai. "Mei's a very optimistic character most of the time, and so we put warm lights on her in contrast with the blue. But when everything is at the darkest moment in the story—when she loses Snowball, when she realizes her coworkers are dead—we put in more of that blue tint and pull the color out so that it reflects her mood."

MEI OUTFIT CONCEPTS

▶ **MEI'S OUTFITS** —The cinematic used many assets from the game, but the needs of the story also required the team to concept new designs like Mei's makeshift gun, snow outfit, and her pajamas. The filmmakers used all these elements to support the theme of the animated short. "Her 'pajama' outfit emphasizes her loneliness and vulnerability in the middle of Antarctica," said former art director Mathias Verhasselt. "Whereas her makeshift gun and snow outfit were designed to emphasize her resourcefulness."

Visual development artist Jungah Lee crafted different concepts of Mei, featuring wardrobes that would reflect her personality. "She is kind and cute, and her clothing should feel friendly and endearing," said Lee. "Mei's original design is blue, and she uses ice, so we wanted to keep some of those colors too, even in her comfy clothes."

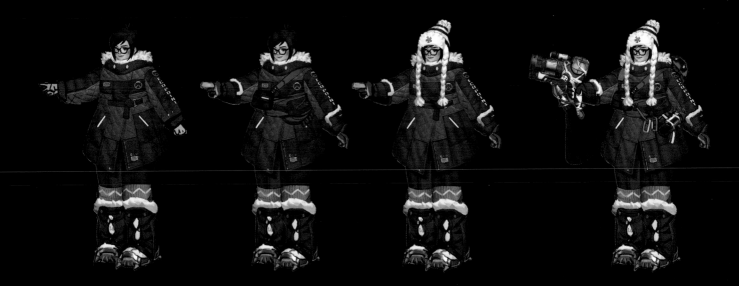

"HONOR AND GLORY"

"Honor and Glory" is a journey into Reinhardt's past and the history of the Overwatch universe. The setting is a battle during the Omnic Crisis, a horrific conflict that pitted humans against robots. For Reinhardt in particular, the specific battle portrayed in "Honor and Glory" changed his life and set him on the path to who he would become.

Released at BlizzCon on November 3, 2017, the film portrays young Reinhardt as a brash and reckless member of Germany's military. "Knowing Reinhardt's character, he likes to smash into big lines of omnics and break through them. I wanted to showcase that in his introduction, so we purposefully designed the moment,"

said the piece's director, Ben Dai. "The sheer amount of effects—there are explosions everywhere. It was a huge amount of effort to do all that. Whenever we put five to ten characters on screen at the same time, it's a challenge."

As the battle unfolds and his actions lead to the death of his mentor, Balderich, he undergoes a transformation— he becomes selfless and learns to put his team above his own pursuit of glory. For the climactic moment of the film, the team used slow motion to draw out the drama in the scenes as much as possible, and to highlight what Reinhardt and Balderich were going through.

NESSKAIN

"One of the themes we wanted to capture was honor—the self-sacrifice of Balderich," said Dai. "We see the young, brash Reinhardt in the beginning, and we show his arc. We showcase that life-changing event where Reinhardt's mentor forfeited his life to save his soldiers and his comrade. He learns the Crusader's job is not about glory—it's about helping and protecting other people."

The team used more desaturated colors than they had for previous cinematics to give the battle a war-movie–feel and to make it seem like it took place in the past. This aesthetic choice also helped differentiate the flashback from the present-day bookend scenes that come at the beginning and end of the film.

Accompanied by Brigitte, Reinhardt is visiting the site of the old battle to pay respects to Balderich and also ponder answering Winston's recall of Overwatch. "What happened in the past is the driving force for Reinhardt," said senior producer Kevin VanderJagt. "It's about remembering the lessons he was taught that define who he is as a character."

YOUNG REINHARDT CONCEPTS

▶ **DESIGNING BALDERICH —**Balderich's armor was inspired by Reinhardt's Lionheart skin. "That look—the more ostentatious and decorative armor overlaid on top of the mech suit—was super cool, and we didn't want to just do that one skin," said Tsang. "When we went to create Balderich, we brought that idea back in. With the Crusaders, we thought they would have done that to their armor—made it more opulent."

"SHOOTING STAR"

"Shooting Star"—revealed on August 22, 2018—tells the story of D.Va and her trusted mechanic, Daehyun, defending Busan from an invasion of Gwishin omnics. Apart from featuring beautiful visual effects and stunning aerial combat, the film also offers a glimpse behind the scenes of one of *Overwatch*'s most popular characters. "Up to that point, D.Va appeared super confident, always wanting to win," said Tsang. "The thing we wanted to show is that, even though she

seems like that on the surface, if you dive deeper, you'll discover she works really hard, and she's very hard on herself." Contrasting visuals were used to show the difference between D.Va in public and in private. At the beginning of the animated short, her face is streaked with grease as she works on her mech in the MEKA base, while in the background, a TV program portrays her as a glamorous superstar living the high life. The creators also relied on dark and cold lighting for most

of the show to emphasize D.Va's belief that much of the responsibility for protecting her country rests on her alone.

D.Va's sense of duty is illustrated when she faces off against an overwhelming force of Gwishin omnics, battling them in an aerial dogfight. "Originally, we planned for most of the combat sequence to happen over the city. And then what happened is it became citywide destruction, which was going to be very challenging to pull off," said the piece's director, Ben Dai. "Omnics crashing into buildings and billboards. Then there are civilians involved. At one point there was even a little girl with a D.Va doll watching the fight happen. But we eventually put it over the ocean because that's the natural geography near D.Va's base."

MANUEL DISCHINGER

This decision required the creators to make choices about what the capabilities of D.Va's mech was. "In the beginning, we were talking about how D.Va's mech functions. In the game, she can only boost for a short time. But in the cinematic, the whole action has to take place on a large body of water, so we couldn't have her hop around—there was nothing to hop on," said Dai. "So we decided that in the shorts, let's give her a little more juice so she can fly the mech around if she wants to."

▶ For "Shooting Star," the creators solicited feedback from a diverse focus group, which included Korean employees. The intent was to ensure cultural authenticity and to gauge whether the portrayal of D.Va and her personal challenges felt genuine. The team gathered a wealth of insightful feedback from the viewers. One of the focus group members compared the hero to a famous Korean ice skater due to her tenacity and demeanor.

▶ **MEKA BASE —**One of the challenges with creating the short was building the MEKA base, where a large part of the story takes place. The location was also being developed as a map for the game, and the members of the team worked very closely to ensure that both versions of the location would be as close to identical as possible. The main difference between the two renditions of the base was the level of detail. Animated shorts can convey higher levels of fidelity than the game engine—textures, architectural detail, and effects are usually more complex.

"The challenge was interpreting the art from the cinematic assets to the game while also maintaining the vision that had been established," said senior environment artist Al Crutchley. "To make it work, we would break down some of the details from those assets but retain the identifying shapes."

Simplifying details is a hallmark of the team's approach to creating environments for the game. Often, they will identify the interesting elements in a prop or piece of architecture, draw those out as the main focal points, and then layer in minor touches for additional texture and flavor.

MEKA SQUAD CONCEPTS

DAE-HYUN FINAL CONCEPT

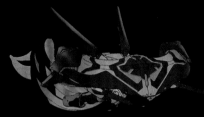

▶ Unlike "Rise and Shine" and "Honor and Glory," D.Va's animated short did not directly tie into Winston's recall. But it did expand *Overwatch*'s lore by fleshing out the Gwishin omnics, showing how different parts of the world face unique threats.

MEKA SQUAD

JAE-EUN **CASINO**

YUNA **D.MON**

HANA **D.VA**

KYUNG-SOO **KING**

SEUNG-HWA **OVERLORD**

MEKA BASE: DAY AND NIGHT

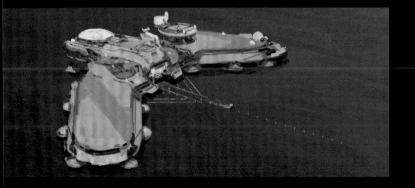

TOP: **MANUEL DISCHINGER**; MIDDLE: **JUNGAH LEE**; BOTTOM: **VASILI ZORIN**

"REUNION"

Released on November 2, 2018, "Reunion" was a departure from previous animated shorts in many ways. It was heavily inspired by classic Western movies, which gave the team an opportunity to create a fun and highly stylized *Overwatch* story incorporating elements from that genre. This also influenced how the team brought color and light into the cinematic.

"It has the aesthetic of a Western. The map was just perfect for that," said director Jason Hill, referring to the Route 66 environment where the story is staged. "It has oranges, reds, and little pops of green from the plants. It all just kind of came together serendipitously."

Unlike the other cinematics, Hill and the team also designed more new characters than they had for previous animated shorts. "Reunion" introduced Ashe, B.O.B., the other members of the Deadlock Gang, and Echo. "There's a moment in TV and films where you see a group of outlaws or bounty hunters and you think, 'These guys are super cool, and I just want to know more about them,'" said Hill. "That's what I really wanted out of the Deadlock Gang. I wanted each one to potentially be a hero—each one could have a story or backstory that we could explore at some point."

To create this feeling for the characters, the team took great care in how they designed the members of the Deadlock Gang. All of them required something different—something *special* that would give them a unique identity.

"Each of the triplets represents one of the races in *StarCraft*," said Tsang, of the three "triplet" members of the Deadlock Gang. "If you look at the tattoos on their shoulders, each has a zerg, protoss, or terran."

TRIPLETS CONCEPT

"REUNION" COLOR KEYS

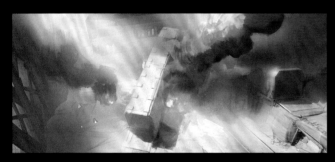

TOP: **JUNGAH LEE** AND **MANUEL DISCHINGER**; BOTTOM: **YEWON PARK AND JAKE PANIA**

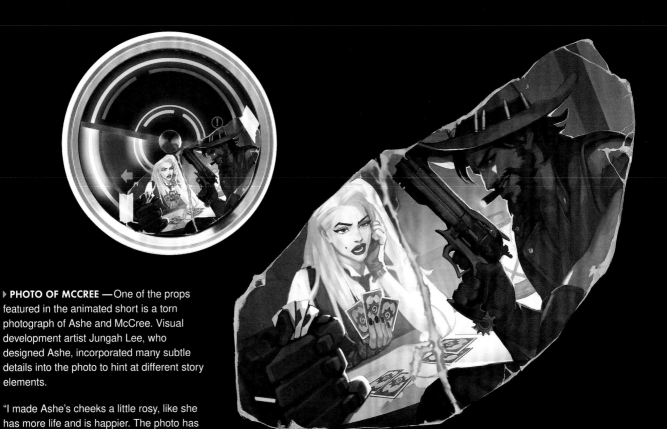

▶ **PHOTO OF MCCREE** —One of the props featured in the animated short is a torn photograph of Ashe and McCree. Visual development artist Jungah Lee, who designed Ashe, incorporated many subtle details into the photo to hint at different story elements.

"I made Ashe's cheeks a little rosy, like she has more life and is happier. The photo has been ripped apart and taped back together," said Lee. "Those little things all tell a story about her."

JUKEBOX ASSEMBLY

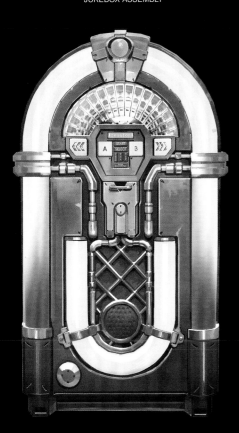

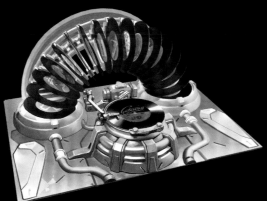

▶ **ECHO AND ASHE** —The original purpose of the cinematic was to introduce and tease a new hero for the game: Echo. However, as the team fleshed out the animated short and created Ashe, they fell in love with her. "It was pretty much unanimous that everyone thought she was a great character, and the team became inspired to make her the next hero instead of Echo," said Jeff Chamberlain.

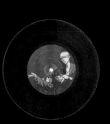

BABS TARR

BEYOND THE GAME

Over the years, the world and characters of *Overwatch* have been represented in many different mediums. Even before the game was released, the developers created a series of comics fleshing out the backstories of some of the heroes.

This trend continued from 2017 on. Apart from just comics, the game and its heroes appeared on toy shelves, breakfast food aisles, bookstores, and more. *Overwatch*'s expanding reach was a sign of its growth and popularity—and also the team's confidence that it had established the game's unique art style.

"Beyond our wildest imaginations, the game blew up. And it was the community of fan artists and cosplayers that took it to the end reaches. There are all these different interpretations of our characters now, and we love it," said character art director Arnold Tsang. "The characters have been imagined in so many ways, we can now be very flexible with how we approach things."

ALBUM COVERS

When the developers began creating albums of *Overwatch*'s music, they wanted to do more than use screenshots or concept art for the covers. They wanted something *unexpected*.

And so they turned to Janice Chu, one of Blizzard's senior UI artists. Before joining the company, she had created *Overwatch* postcards as well as isometric dioramas of a fictional turn-based *Overwatch* strategy game. "At first we were thinking about the postcard images. Some of the early versions of the album covers were more like that. But at some point, looking at her isometric art, we thought those would be really unique as well," said Tsang.

The postcard style would have worked perfectly for the first album: *Cities & Countries*. But the team was also planning on creating a *Heroes & Villains* and an *Animated Shorts* album. They pivoted to the isometric art style since it would create a cohesive visual theme between all the soundtrack covers.

JANICE CHU

LÚCIO-OH'S BOX ART

The initial idea for Lúcio-Oh's started as a spray made by Aquatic Moon, an art house that the team has worked with over the years to create in-game content. "They were just jamming on ideas for sprays and they did this randomly," said Tsang. "It was very specific—Lúcio-Oh's instead of Lúci-O's."

Later, when the possibility of partnering with Kellogg's to create a cereal came up, the team naturally gravitated toward turning the spray into something real. When it came to designing the box, the team considered a few different possibilities. "For the cereal, we could have easily had 3-D renders of the characters, but I think 2-D art really captures a certain life to the heroes," said Tsang.

Visual concept artist Manuel Deschinger created different poses for Lúcio to find the right image that would capture his energy. When the team finally announced the product at BlizzCon, it was even accompanied by a commercial starring Lúcio's voice actor, Johnny Cruz.

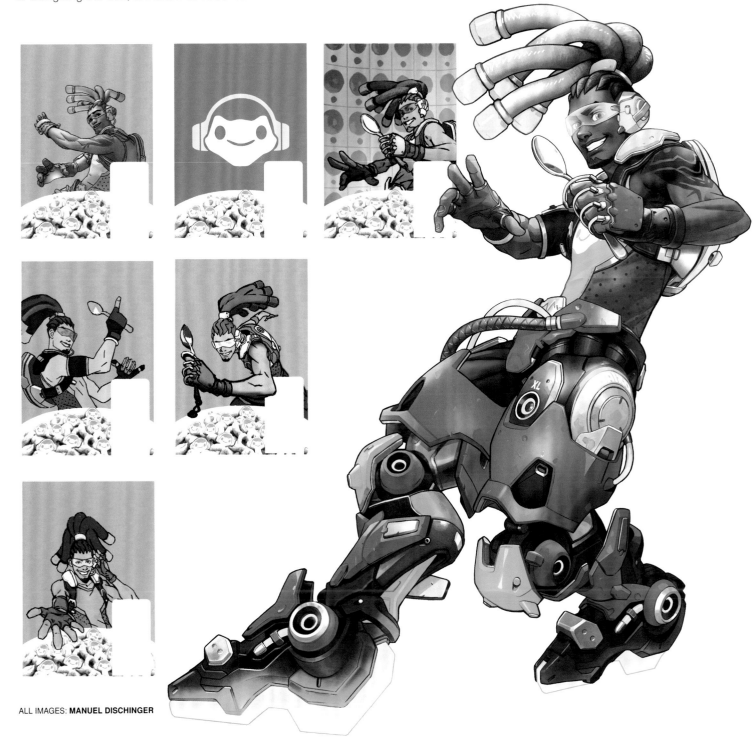

ALL IMAGES: **MANUEL DISCHINGER**

COMIC AND BOOK ART

▶ **HERO OF NUMBANI COVER** —For the cover of the young adult novel *The Hero of Numbani*, the team partnered with artist Odera Igbokwe to depict the brilliant roboticist Efi and her creation, Orisa. As with the comics creators the designers had partnered with, they were open to exploration. They wanted Igbokwe's unique style informed by Afro-diasporic mythology and Afrofuturism to interpret Overwatch and its characters in a new light. "People that we work with, we already feel like if they were to draw in their natural style, it would fit under the Overwatch umbrella stylistically," said Tsang.

They treated the piece as an illustration, which opened the door for more stylistic exploration. "When you're doing concept art or promotional art, you want to stick to the model one-to-one as much as you can," said Tsang. "But with an illustration, there's more room for interpretation."

ODERA IGBOKWE

Since *Overwatch*'s announcement in 2014, the team has released comics exploring the game world and its heroes. Some of these stories focus on adventures undertaken by the characters, like *Train Hopper*, written by Robert Brooks with art by Bengal.

Reflections, written by Michael Chu and illustrated by Miki Montlló, gave players a glimpse into heroes' personal lives and revealed Tracer as the game's first LGBTQ+ character.

TOP LEFT & RIGHT: **MIKI MONTLLÓ**; BOTTOM LEFT: **BENGAL**

TOP ROW: **BENGAL**; BOTTOM LEFT: **BABS TARR**; BOTTOM MIDDLE: **GGDG**; BOTTOM RIGHT: **ZOE THOROGOOD**

For these comics as well as book covers, the developers have worked with many different artists. All of them have brought a unique style to the content they made. Bengal's use of direct light on characters and environments created vibrant colors in his comic panels. Philippe Colin, who worked on the unreleased Project Titan, was also a master of creating beautifully saturated images.

"A lot of his designs inspired what *Overwatch* came to be," said Tsang of Colin, who also goes by Gray Shuko. "He has this way of designing buildings, vehicles, and props that is futuristic and cool but also has a whimsical side of it—a very inviting feel."

What drew the team to Babs Tarr, who was the artist on the *Tracer—London Calling* comic series, was her understanding of character and motion. Her ability to create compelling poses and action panels was especially important for a story involving the highly kinetic Tracer.

TOP ROW: **BENGAL**; BOTTOM LEFT: **JEN BARTEL**; BOTTOM RIGHT: **SANFORD GREENE**

A GLIMPSE OF THINGS TO COME

The developers had a grand vision for *Overwatch 2*. They wanted to branch out beyond *Overwatch* and explore new heroes, environments, and types of gameplay. One of the biggest additions to the sequel was its emphasis on in-game storytelling: *Overwatch 2* would prominently feature an action-packed and emotionally riveting PVE campaign.

"There's a whole bunch of fans who don't even play *Overwatch*. They might be apprehensive about a competitive game or a PVP experience," said character art director Arnold Tsang. "With *Overwatch 2*, we have the opportunity to bring those people into the fold—people who might really like the art or the characters or watching the animated shorts or cosplay, but who never touched the game because they're not into PVP shooters."

Creating a meaningful PVE campaign, new competitive gameplay, and all of *Overwatch 2*'s other features forced the developers to ask themselves a familiar question: *How are we going to do it?*

"When we first started, we didn't think of redesigning the characters because we were very precious about how they were represented," said Tsang. "We thought if we messed with them, they wouldn't be recognizable anymore."

But as time passed, the idea of exploring fresh looks for the characters seemed like a necessary *and* exciting opportunity. The team reimagined the heroes in many ways, such as by creating more layers for their costumes and outfitting them in high-tech materials. "That made the characters feel more sophisticated, and it allowed us to show off more material definition that wasn't possible in the first *Overwatch*," said Tsang. "For example, Tracer is so iconic that we didn't want to change her too much, but we evolved her leather jacket to a tech-wear waterproof windbreaker that has more intricate straps and buckles."

Not all heroes were approached the same way as Tracer. For Genji, the designers created an outfit that he could wear over his cybernetic body. This new wardrobe was originally designed by visual development artist Jungah Lee for the *Overwatch 2* announcement cinematic, "Zero Hour," and then adapted for the game engine.

Hair was another impactful way to freshen up the characters' appearances. "In real life, when you change your hairstyle, it's like you're a new person," said Tsang. "Sometimes we did something drastic, and sometimes it was more subtle. For Widowmaker, we changed her long ponytail into more of a French braid." The team had different technology to leverage for these changes than it had in the past. With *Overwatch*, the hair was sculpted into solid geometric shapes, but now the designers could create more realistic textures, where actual strands of hair would be visible.

The heroes weren't the only part of the game that would undergo significant aesthetic changes. The developers would harness other new techniques and technologies to create maps that were even more dynamic than before. Building on the hurricane they had made for the Storm Rising Archives event, the developers would explore other unique types of weather and atmospheric effects.

For every aspect of the sequel, the answer to *"How are we going to do it?"* would be different—unique solutions to unique situations. But the developers would find a way forward by breaking boundaries, learning from the past, collaborating, and championing *Overwatch*'s diversity, hope, and bright future.

That was how they did it for the content featured in this book, and that is how they would do it again for *Overwatch 2*.

ORIGINAL TRACER

OVERWATCH 2 TRACER

ORIGINAL WIDOWMAKER

OVERWATCH 2 WIDOWMAKER

ALL IMAGES: **ARNOLD TSANG**